Tassels

Tassels

Susan Dickens

Illustrations by Jane Devine

Photography by Neil Lorimer

A SUE HINES BOOK

ALLEN & UNWIN

First published in 2000
A Sue Hines Book
Allen & Unwin Pty Ltd
9 Atchison Street
St Leonards NSW 1590
Australia
Phone: (61 2) 8425 0100
Fax: (61 2) 9906 2218
E-mail: frontdesk@allen-unwin.com.au
Web: http://www.allen-unwin.com.au

National Library of Australia
Cataloguing-in-Publication entry:

Dickens, Susan, 1943–.
Tassels.
ISBN 1 86508 081 0.
1. Tassels. I. Lorimer, Neil. II. Devine, Jane. III. Title.
746.27

Illustrations by Jane Devine
Photography by Neil Lorimer
Designed and typeset by text-art
Printed in China by Everbest Printing Co. Ltd.

Contents

Introduction

Since my book the *Art of Tassel Making* was published in 1994,
I have learnt so much more about techniques and the
methods of teaching.

I am convinced there is no greater way to learn than to teach.
If there is a problem you have to solve it, and after a short
time you realise the answer lies in simplifying the method
rather than correcting a mistake.

This book revises techniques and fills gaps as well as
expanding ideas to inspire beginners and those
already proficient in the art of tassel making.

Generally there are two separate areas of tassel making. The
first is concerned with interior design. Tassels made for this
purpose tend to be strong, with bold, clean lines and
minimal decoration. The second area of tassel making is

concerned with the decorative arts. These tassels are richly imagined and display the outstanding skill of their makers. Tassels in this latter group are increasingly used in fashion as decorative additions.

Fashion books in the 1860s featured tassels on capes, hoods, scarves, sashes, parasols, gloves and shoes. Designer Paul Poiret announced that the corset should be banished and presented the bra along with designs for loose robes of fluid lines and with elegant tasselled cords. Poiret's brilliant young Russian assistant Romain de Tiroff (R.T.) 'Erte' greatly influenced the use and style of tassels. He moved to America where William Randolph Hearst hired him to design covers for *Harper's Bazaar*. He worked there for over twenty years and his influence on the lavish use of tassels on clothing, jewellery, accessories, furniture, interiors, theatre costumes and film sets was stunningly imaginative.

The use of tassels in fashion is coming back into vogue. In this book I have included several tassels of this kind.

CHAPTER 1

History

Passementerie is the general term given to cords, braids, tassels and trimmings for use mainly on furnishings and clothing. Its most primitive origins have been traced by archaeologists to the tombs of the Egyptian Pharaohs 5000 years ago.

The tale of the tassel twists and tangles like a thread weaving intricate and colourful patterns through the history of civilisation. From its humble beginnings as a way of stopping a woven cloth from fraying, the methods improved, and ornamentation and complexity grew, echoing influences of different cultures. Each step reflected a development in materials, tastes and, later, influences of economic and political conditions.

Nomadic tribes for centuries fashioned tassels from every conceivable material, animal, vegetable and mineral. These simple tassels represented equal importance to their culture as formal tassels to more sophisticated societies.

Fringing appeared at the same time in Arabia and Polynesia (skirts made of vegetable fibre, feathers, shells); Brazilians and Indians added beads. Egyptians introduced cotton and linen.

Manuscripts from the Byzantine Empire of Constantine record tassels as an important part of early Christian dress. Silk was introduced from China to the Occidental world in the mid-sixth century, providing a luxury fibre for cloth making and, in turn, a delightful material to be used for the focal point of the dress of that time.

Formal tassels probably originated in China, where they have been recorded attached to the tiny painfully bound feet of Chinese women.

During the Middle Ages Christian monks decorated manuscripts with illuminated records highlighting the popularity and importance given to the tassel. They were used to decorate, among other things, clothing, interiors of dwellings, bridles and canopies. Materials used were wool and cotton.

The Arab world, Moorish North Africa and Ottoman Turkey influenced the Spanish who adapted and modified the ornate Islamic style to suit the wealthy Spaniard's taste in clothing and furnishings around the eleventh century.

The Italians enthusiastically adopted new developments in fabulous silk trimmings, and during the Renaissance splendid examples adorned the homes of the wealthy. The church heavily embellished their vestments. Ornamental trims became a badge of wealth and power.

Italian masters of the decorative craft belonged to the Medici court, so when Catherine of Medici moved to France, she took with her their knowledge of weaving and silk dyeing.

European kings and princes had a passion for surrounding themselves with silk and gold (the influence of the Turkish artisans in the Suleiman Empire). It was the French who embraced the art and transported it to its magnificent height in the seventeenth and eighteenth centuries. Evidence of the extravagant excess of Kings Louis XIV (the Sun King, so named because of his love of gold), XV and XVI can still be viewed at the Palace of Versailles.

By the end of the seventeenth century the French had become the masters of the art of passementerie, with abundant embellishments added to, for example, furniture, curtains, tapestries, pillows, clothes and edging on coaches. In Lyon, the capital of the textile industry in Europe, there was an explosion in the development of techniques. A guild was formed for the express purpose of protecting highly valued French artisans.

With the French Revolution towards the end of the eighteenth century, there was a brief lapse in the popularity of passementerie when excess of any kind in dress and decoration was banned.

Napoleon brought with him in the early 1800s an insatiable appetite for golden embellishment and rekindled the passion for flamboyantly tasselled decorations. Josephine, at Malmaison, busied herself with a new breed of artist, The Interior Decorator. Together, Charles Percier and Pierre Fontain created an imperial style complete with tents and tasselled flagpoles.

The post-revolution era saw a period when persons of wealth surrounded themselves with the most fabulous adornment, which was used to enhance the status of the military, the Church and royalty.

Lyon again became the centre, this time for gold and silver thread production. Passementerie houses were flooded with orders from all over the world, for military and ecclesiastical, as well as furnishing and clothing, requirements.

In 1815 the Jacquard loom revolutionised the production of braids, ribbons and fringe. These huge machines required special housing with high roofs and enormous windows. Because of the loom's efficiency many of the hand-workers were made redundant.

During the eighteenth and nineteenth centuries the tassel industry burgeoned further. Tassels had been in production in England since the Huguenots

brought from France their skills as weavers in the seventeenth and eighteenth centuries, and during the Victorian era tassels and trims were lavishly used.

America too, was seduced by the charm of passementerie, and many firms had been established by 1800. Samandre is one of the few original tassel houses to survive today.

Experiments were made with new materials during the nineteenth century Art Nouveau period, with the advent of synthetic silk-like fibre. Later, in the 1920s, when Art Deco lines became clean and uncluttered by ornamentation, the fringed skirt and tasselled additions to capes, bags, and hats served as a swinging visual reminder of the mood and movement of the times.

Few houses remain working according to old traditions, using old tools. In the Valley of Dorlay where the passementerie factories were relocated from the centre, Lyon, there were many factories lining the banks of the river. Only one remains today as a museum.

In France in 1960 there were forty large factories in production; today two-thirds have gone, and in the future there will be even less. Though there is competition there is a family spirit of community binding the remaining groups. Among their clientele today are the interior decorator, the exporter of a catalogue range to overseas countries, haute couture trims and designer houses.

Some examples have survived for us to see today, and to marvel at the wonder of the intricately fine work. It reflects the subtlety of the artisan's hand and a creative spirit, combined with the use of more fragile materials to breathe depth into the work that machines are at a loss to replicate.

CHAPTER 2

Equipment

Here are some notes on materials and equipment to get you
started. You need minimal formal equipment to make the tassels
in this book—thread is the vital ingredient. Many of the
items I use are easily found around the house.

You will need the following materials to make a tassel based on a form.

thread, ribbon, gimp (see glossary)
warping board
cardboard card or cylinder on which to wind
    prepared skirt thread to hold it ready for use
scissors
templates
needles—a wool needle, milliners needle no. 9,
    no. 3, beading needles
wire
wire cutters
sharp-nosed pliers
masking or adhesive tape
tape measure
form or mould
wooden beads of various sizes and shapes
adhesive—spray and tube
anchorage
winding device
combs and steam

*extra items are required for specific decoration—they are included where needed

THREAD

The variety of thread available for tassel making is vast and confusing to the beginner, but after a little practice and experimentation you will be comfortable working with and managing large volumes of thread. The brands and colours of thread in each design are recommended as a guide only. Provided that the ply is of similar weight, experiment with your own colours and materials.

Small tassels such as key tassels and those used for garment ornamentation can be made from embroidery thread such as DMC Perle cottons, YLI silk floss or Australian Gumnut Yarns, pure silk, cotton and wool hand-dyed yarns. Large tassels traditionally used as curtain tiebacks will require much more thread; many varieties are suitable or combinations of different thread may be used.

In Australia (Melbourne) Taxtor Trading, wholesalers of bulk yarn, will cone together x 6 ends. Provided the same yarn is selected they will mix colours. This reduces the amount of warping.

Yeoman Yarns in the UK has a large range of threads suitable for tassels (see page 135 for a list of suppliers).

The materials I have found successful for tassel making are:

perle thread
balls of crochet thread
Benz and YLI Pearl Crown Rayon (100 m/110 yards
    cones)
rayon high-twist yarn
weaving thread
knitting yarn
chenille knitting yarn
linen thread
Madeira tanne cotton
gimp cord (thin covered cord rather than a thread)
jute
embroidery wool, cotton and silk

Sewing yarn is also needed. I use Nymo, a fine linear thread with no twist. Nymo comes in various weights from 000, the finest, to D, the strongest. The advantage of using Nymo is that it neither breaks nor slips. (Ribbon, as well as wooden, glass or ceramic beads, and feathers are all useful additions to thread for tassels.)

WARPING BOARD

Thread is prepared on a warping board to make the tassel skirt, cord, rope and ruffs.

Warped threads are those which have been wound around two or more stable objects evenly tensioned to result in several threads or 'ends' to be used as you would use one.

The length of board is fitted with dowels or posts to enable the thread to be 'warped' to a suitable length to make the tassel skirt and ropes.

There are many types of warping boards or

Tools and materials required for tassel making.

Various threads used in tassel making.

Forms used in tassel making.

Equipment needed for making the skirts.

frames on the market, obtainable from craft shops specialising in weaving materials. A long length of pine board with dowels fixed in each end is an inexpensive alternative.

The size I find most convenient is 1.5 m (1 ¾ yards) long and 35 cm (14 in) wide with four posts each end enabling me to warp skirt lengths of 10.5 m

(12 ½ yards) and rope lengths of approx 2.5 m (2 ¾ yards) (when finished) (figures 2.1, 2.2, 2.3).

The dowels also serve as 'posts' when anchorage is required (see page 9).

The alternative to a warping board is the backs of two chairs set apart to give the required length between (figure 2.4).

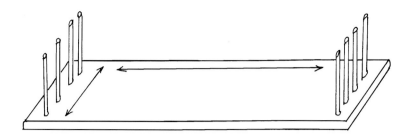

Figure 2.1

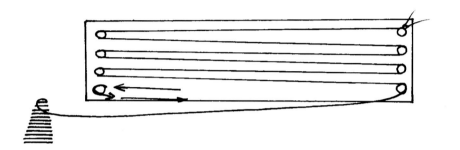

Figure 2.2

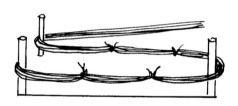

Figure 2.3

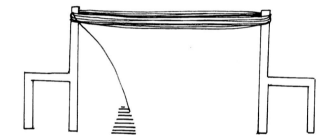

Figure 2.4

SCISSORS

Sharp scissors are essential for cutting the skirt from the board and the final trimming of the skirt. A serrated edge grips the thread well.

You will need utility scissors for paper or wire cutting.

TEMPLATES

SKIRT

A firm solid cardboard (not corrugated) template equal to the required length of the skirt is necessary, unless you have a formal set of varying sized wooden boards. The wooden ones are comfortable to use but the end result is no different from that of the cardboard.

RUFF

The curled ruff is made on a knitting needle, pencil or piece of dowel, depending on the thickness of the loops or curls required.

The thick velvet or fluffy ruff is best made on a small template made by cutting two 3 cm (1 ⅛ in) square pieces of fine corrugated cardboard separated by two satay sticks (see figure 7.6).

A fine cut ruff would be made on a knitting needle, pencil or piece of wooden dowel.

WIRE

Fine wire such as hobby or craft wire bought from a hardware store is used to hold the skirt threads in place. You may use beading wire but it is more expensive.

Aluminium wire of 1.6 gauge holds the rope at the top of, and runs through the centre hole in, the form.

Wire cutting snippers or old scissors are used to cut the skirt wire.

Sharp-nosed pliers are necessary to turn thicker gauge wire to lock the rope to the base of the form.

FORM OR MOULD

Most often used is a single wooden form (or mould). A variety of different shaped wooden sections covered, then joined by a central wire, makes a complex shape. Figure 2.5 shows wooden forms used in this book.

More contemporary examples are made using metal, resin, ceramic, tin, cardboard or papier-mâché.

Soft top tassels are made with fringing and allow for embroidery embellishment.

Large beads are sometimes used as an element of the tassel form. See details of bead shapes and sizes on page 10.

ADHESIVE

Spray or some form of strong impact adhesive is used to hold the covering in place on the form and on large beads and rope dividers. I have found 3M Multi-Purpose spray adhesive to be both waterproof and heat resistant.

Quick Grip is a good, all-purpose glue.

Superglue is for use on spun wire flowers and the ends of separate lengths of bullion twists for tassel skirts.

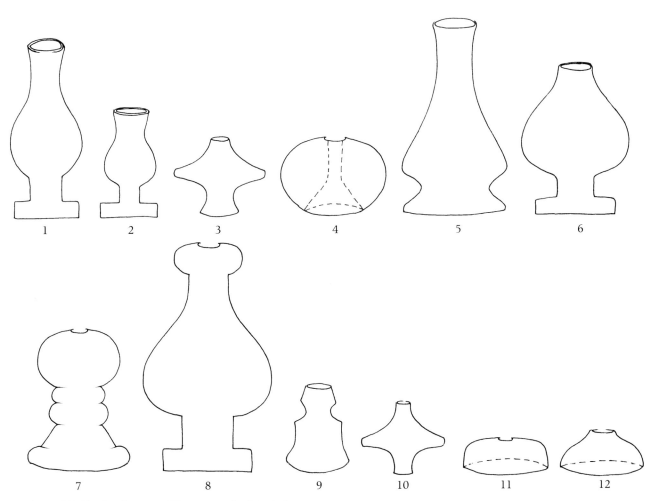

Figure 2.5 Wooden forms, at 50 per cent of original size

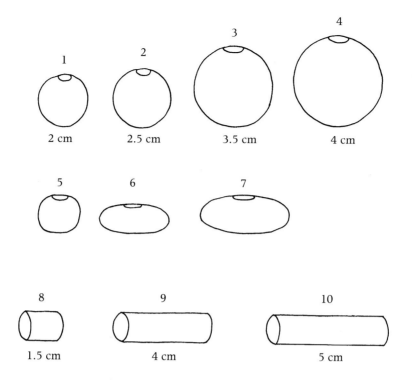

Figure 2.6 Beads

ANCHORAGE

A tight-fitting drawer or G-clamp is needed for rope making. I have some great pump action grips with posts, which come in a variety of sizes and are obtainable from hardware stores. The type I have is called Quick Grip.

A firm anchorage, such as a wooden bobbin clamped to the table, is necessary to hold the tassel in a stable and comfortable position while adding embellishments. A chopstick or dowel is set in a hole in the centre for the tassel head to sit on. The stick may need a piece of cling wrap or tape, so the head sits firmly and the tassel is stable.

You may substitute a square of wood with a hole drilled through the centre into which a wooden dowel is glued.

WINDING DEVICE

The most basic winding device is a pencil or chopstick used with a cardboard cylinder; next is a battery-operated drill. (Electric drills go too fast to control and do not have a reverse action.) Best of all is a cabler or cord winding device which will twist up to four segments of cord at once.

COMB AND STEAM

A wide-toothed comb and steam will remove any kinks and crinkles from the skirt before its final trim.

A carding comb is useful to finish pompoms and onion tassels. Better still is a special little metal brush known as a 'turkey' brush which fits over your index finger. A hard toothbrush will do the job if nothing else is available.

Steam the finished tassel over a boiling kettle or saucepan to remove kinks, taking care not to scald your hands.

CHAPTER 3

Anatomy of a Tassel

Tassel making is similar to dress design: you are in fact dressing a shape. So your approach is the same—you consider the basic shape you are to cover, and the style, materials and colour to be used to suit the setting.

Unlike dressmaking there is usually very little sewing involved; in its place is winding, spinning, wrapping, wiring and gluing.

It is important to begin by understanding the parts that make up a tassel. Generally there are four main components:

- the cord or rope
- the form or mould
- the skirt section
- the ruff.

It is best to understand the basics of these four parts before moving to more complicated variations and embellishments. It will become clear as you become familiar with these principles that these methods are interchangeable. Finally, be aware that tassel making is very forgiving.

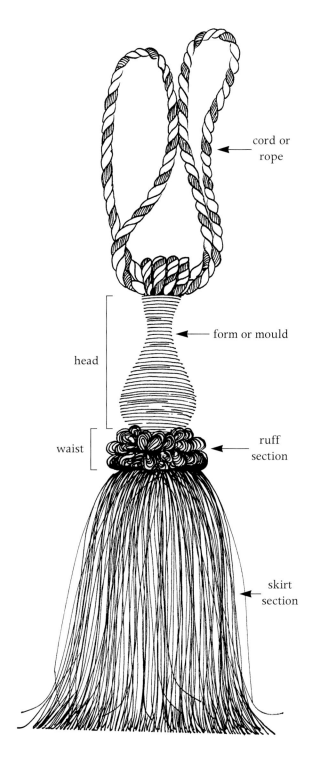

cord or rope

form or mould

head

waist

ruff section

skirt section

CHAPTER 4

Rope and Cord Making

Cords and rope are similar. When I refer to a cord, I mean something thinner and used for small tassels, or a part of something bigger. The term rope is used when referring to a suspension for a large tassel.

There are quite sophisticated rope making devices on the market today, and if you are planning to make a career in passementerie you simply could not live without one, but for the occasional tassel maker a chopstick, and a firm fitting drawer, will be sufficient.

In this section four methods are described: hand twisting;

using a battery-operated drill; using a cylinder to assist hand twisting; and using a cabler.

Originally all thread begins as filament without any twist. To make it manageable for whatever use, it has to be spun to give it strength and order. It is then plied with two or three similar thicknesses. This is usually the state in which we find our material.

Some thread has a higher twist than others, which means the original twist before the thread is plied has been spun very tightly. High twist yarns work wonderfully for tassels as the higher the twist, the less tangles remain in the skirt as it moves.

- *Primary twist* is the first twist of the **warp** (see glossary, page 133).
- *Plying* is the twisting back after joining two or more primary twisted warps.
- *Even balance* means the segments have twisted back to a neutral state after plying (equal to about half the primary twist). Any further twisting on would overtwist to start another primary twist.

There are two types of rope—simple and complex:

- *Simple* is when there has been only one primary twist followed by a plying twist.
- *Complex* is when two or more plied cords are twisted on again with a second primary twist and joined by plying back together.

You make complex rope when you wish to create a mix of colour, to make patterns within the length of either texture or colour.

The more twists and plies the segments have the stronger, harder, thicker and shorter the sections will become.

S AND Z TWIST

The basis of all cords and ropes is the S twist (clockwise) and the Z twist (anticlockwise).

To make a Z twist, take two or more segments of equal length and thickness. Twist them separately

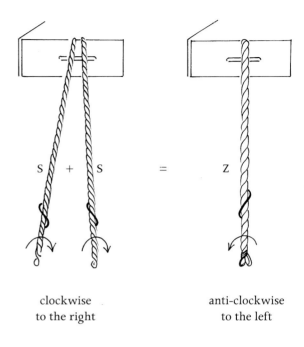

clockwise
to the right

anti-clockwise
to the left

Figures 4.1, 4.2

the same number of times in a clockwise direction (figure 4.1). This is an S twist. Join the segments and let them twist back on the anticlockwise direction (figure 4.3). This is a Z twist.

To make an S twist, twist the segments separately the same number of times in an anticlockwise direction (figure 4.2). This is Z. Join the segments and let them twist back in a clockwise direction (figure 4.4). This is S.

It sounds really confusing, but after you have twisted up a few you can *see* rather than *think* your way through. When making simple cords and ropes it is of no importance in which rotation the cord is spun.

When you want different patterns with colour or texture variations, which require varying segment sizes to be combined, a good understanding of S and Z is necessary. As well you need an accurate record of the thread count and number of twists. The variations and combinations are enormous, and I will give examples of just a few.

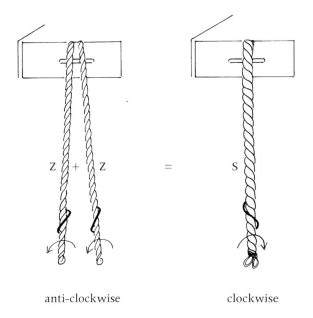

Z + Z = S

anti-clockwise   clockwise

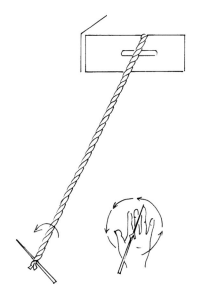

Figures 4.3, 4.4

SIMPLE KINK-TWISTED CORD—
ONE COLOUR

a warp of yarn
winding device—for example a pencil or
    chopstick
adhesive tape
anchorage

- Knot each end of thread.
- Anchor one knotted end to a post or jam the
  end into tight fitting drawer (figure 4.5).
- Separate free end and position pencil close to
  knot.
- Hold firmly with one hand with thread
  between the first two fingers and hard against
  pencil (see detail of figure 4.5). Spin pencil
  with the other hand, keeping the warp taut.
  Maintain the tension and twist until the thread
  becomes tight and firm, wanting to twist back
  onto itself.

Figure 4.5

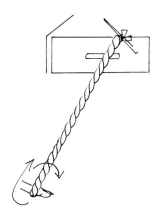

Figure 4.6

- Fold in half and let cord twist back onto itself
  (figure 4.6).
- Stretch and tighten to eliminate any kinks.
- Tape the two free ends together.

SIMPLE KINK-TWISTED CORD—
TWO COLOURS

Short cords with finished ends are suitable for skirt
bullions (see glossary, page 133). These short cords

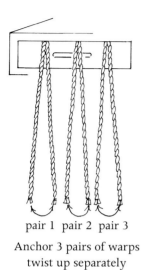

pair 1 pair 2 pair 3

Anchor 3 pairs of warps
twist up separately

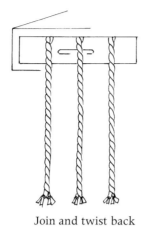

Join and twist back

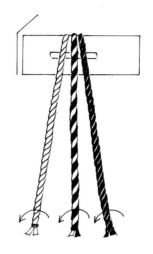

Figure 4.12a, b

Figures 4.14, 4.15

Step 1

- Anchor the 3 pairs of warps.
- Twist up each pair in turn (figure 4.12) with a primary twist, then ply back together (figure 4.13). Secure ends with tape.
- You will now have 3 cords.

Step 2

- In turn twist on each cord to tighten until ready to kink back on itself, maintaining the tension as each is twisted (figure 4.14).
- Tape the three segments together and twist back to an even balance (figure 4.15). Tape the other end and remove from the anchor.

FOUR-PART DOUBLE-TWISTED WITH MIXED COLOURS

4 pairs of equal warps, 2 pairs matched colours and 2 pairs mixed
winding device
masking tape

Example A

- Attach 4 warps to the anchor, in alternating order (figure 4.16). Primary twist each one separately until tight (figure 4.17).
- Ply back to make 4 cords, and twist on to tighten. Maintain tension on each cord as it is twisted (figure 4.18).

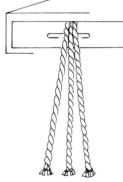

Twist on 3 pairs of
cords

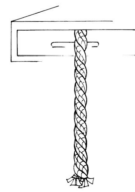

Join and twist back
to make a double
twisted 3 segment
rope using 1 colour

Figure 4.13a, b

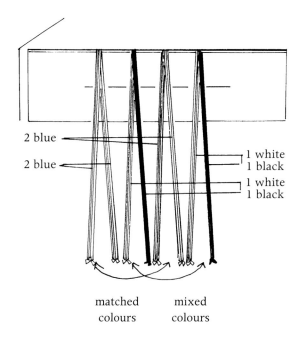

2 blue

2 blue

1 white
1 black

1 white
1 black

matched
colours

mixed
colours

Figure 4.16

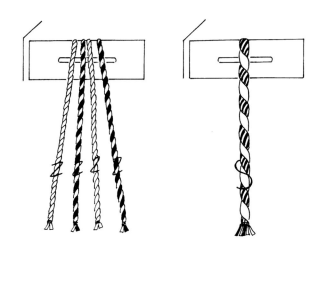

Figures 4.18, 4.19

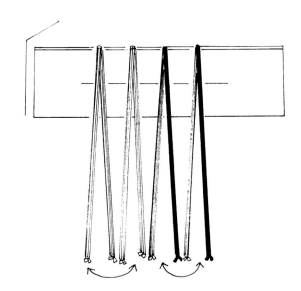

Figure 4.17

Figure 4.20

- Join the 4 segments and ply back to result in a simple alternating colour pattern (figure 4.19).

Example B

- Attach all the warps to the anchor, matching pairs together (figure 4.20) and repeat as above

for example A (figures 4.21, 4.22).
- When the segments are joined and plied you will have 2 pairs of plain colours and 2 mixed pairs spiralling together (figure 4.23).
- The variations in colour patterns to be mixed and matched are endless.

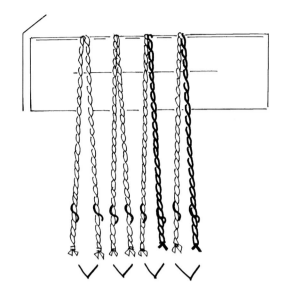

Figure 4.21

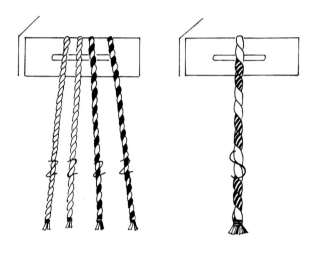

Figures 4.22, 4.23

Spun Cord

Often on expensive tassels the ropes are made from large gimp segments. (Gimp has a centre core of cotton and has been spun over with a fine thread (often filament rayon), sometimes using a blend of different colours seen within the main body of the tassel.) The end result is a very hard stiff rope. This process is not easy, but it is possible for the enthusiastic person to try, and once mastered is very satisfying.

This principle is used also when spinning up wire and metal strips for embellishments.

It needs to be done with a battery-operated drill; don't use an electric drill as they can go out of control and have no reverse action.

2 people
2 m (2⅖ yards) x 10 ends cotton warp core
covering thread to cover (for example rayon)
post with a swivel (try a fishing shop; make sure
    the swivel runs well; WD40 spray loosens old
    ones from the bottom of fishing tackle baskets)
15 cm (6 in) linen thread
battery-operated drill

- Knot each end of the cotton warp.
- Attach the swivel to the post by tying securely using about 15 cm (6 in) of linen thread.
- Tie one end of the core thread to the swivel so it will spin freely without interfering with the spin of the swivel. Attach the other end of the core thread to the chuck of the drill (you may fix a cup hook into the drill, then loop the knotted end of the thread over the hook).
  I simply tape a piece of masking tape with the covering thread I am to use, make a couple of knots, then lock the lot into the chuck.
- Pinch the cotton warp and attached rayon thread close to the drill chuck firmly (be sure the thread is free to run), switch the drill on and move your hand smoothly along the warp so there is an even cover of thread spun over the warp. You might need to practise this a couple of times before you feel comfortable.
- Tape both ends with masking tape before cutting free.

CHAPTER 5

Nina

This is the easiest tassel to make.

The three-part twisted rope enters the top.

The outside of the wooden form is sprayed twice with an adhesive spray, then covered with fine gimp.

The skirt is simple and straight. There is a curled ruff at the waist where the skirt has been attached.

Many of the other tassels have this tassel as the base with added embellishments. Some of the proceeding tassels will refer back to methods for this one.

5 YLI reels 100 m (110 yards) Pearl Crown Rayon:

    1 x no. 103 (peach), 2 x no. 811 (old rose),

    2 x no. 319 (drab green)

7 m (7¾ yards) Mokuba Gimp (old rose)

wooden form no. 1

1.5 m (1⅔ yards) hobby wire

15 cm (6 in) 1.6 gauge aluminium wire

THE FORM

form no. 1

7 m (7¾ yards) gimp

chopstick

15 cm (6 in) cling wrap

scissors

cotton thread to wind around the waist

- Wrap the piece of cling wrap over the chop-stick to provide a base onto which the form fits snugly. Lift the bottom edge of the film, and wrap around the base of the form to protect it from being sprayed (figure 5.1); do not let film cover any part of the head of the form.

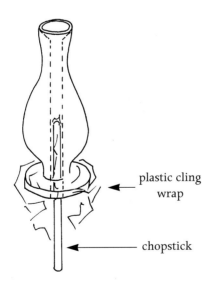

plastic cling wrap

chopstick

Figure 5.1

- Using a high quality aerosol spray adhesive, finely coat the head, including just inside the lip at the top and the curved underside of the head (figure 5.2).

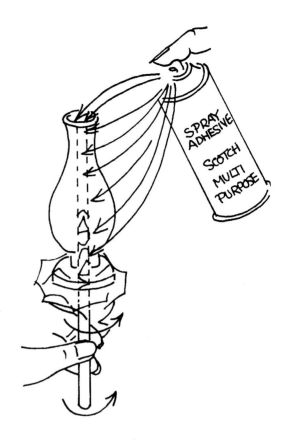

Figure 5.2

- Allow to dry approximately 3 minutes. Apply second fine coat. Allow to dry a further 3 minutes until surface becomes 'high tack'.
- Take one free end of the gimp, place just inside the lip of the form (not down the hole). Press with tip of finger to bond. Twist chopstick with one hand, and with the other, guide the gimp around the lip to form the first coil (figure 5.3).
- Twist further to form three more coils before firming, and bond the gimp to the head with fingers (taking care not to touch the sticky surface).
- Hold gimp taut with one hand, twist with the other, keeping each coil close and parallel to the one above so as to conceal the wood beneath.
- Continue to twist, carefully guiding the gimp until the head is covered.

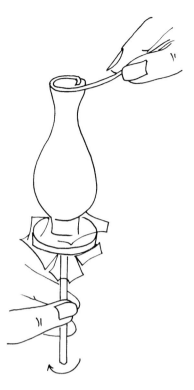

Figure 5.3

- It is easiest to invert the form when half covered. Don't tension the gimp when going 'downhill', just press lightly with fingertips to bond.
- Finish at the junction of the head with the waist by cutting gimp flush with the form.
- Remove plastic wrap and stick. Wind a band of cotton thread around the waist (figure 5.4).

Figure 5.4

THE SKIRT

Enough skirt should be made to twice fit around the waist. As the skirt is worked the template fills from left to right. A small scalloped edge forms at the top edge of the board and a neat row of wire is visible just beneath. You will need to pass 3 ends (peach, rose and green) 10 times over a 9 m (10 yards) measure, then 2 ends (rose and green) once more to give 32 ends.

To make the skirt:
9 m (10 yards) warp x 32 ends rayon thread, peach, old rose, drab green
10 cm (4 in) skirt template
1.5 m (1 ⅔ yards) hobby wire
masking tape
scissors (sharp)

- Double the wire in half and twist a loop at the fold (figure 5.5 a, b).

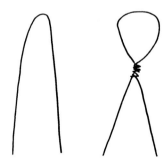

Figure 5.5a, b

- Place warp thread between the wire against the twist, leaving a 10 cm (4 in) tail. Twist wires tightly about 3 times to secure the thread to the wire (figure 5.6).
- Tape the free end of the warp to the back of the template on the lower left-hand edge (figure 5.7).
- Position the attached wire and warp at the top left-hand edge of the template, with one wire lying down the face of the template, and the other lying down the back (figure 5.8).

- Follow the method for the simple hand-twisted 3-part rope on page 16.

To attach the wire to the rope:
rope
15 cm (6 in) 1.6 aluminium wire
sharp-nosed pliers
wool needle
strong sewing thread

- Thread a wool needle with 1.5 m (1 ⅔ yards) strong thread.
- Make small closed loop at one end of the wire using the pliers.
- Sandwich the looped end of the wire between the two rope ends, about 1.5 cm (⅔ in) above the taped end (figure 5.15).

Figure 5.16

Figure 5.15

- Sew through the rope segments and looped end of wire 3 times one side, then 3 times the other, to be sure the wire is attached firmly (figure 5.16). Then neatly and firmly bind the ropes tightly together with the wire, just below the loop of the wire, about 6 to 8 times.
- Trim the taped ends from the rope to make as neat as possible, close to the bound area, with small sharp scissors (figure 5.17).
- Make a simple overhand knot, and work it down to sit over the binding. Sew in position to make a firm, neat little knob. Make the

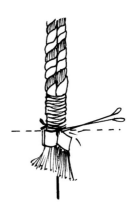

Figure 5.17

stitches disappear by sewing between the grooves of the rope.

To attach the rope to the tassel:
- Thread the tassel head on to the wire. Cup the knot in the palm of the hand and support the head securely with the fingers. Invert the tassel.
- Take the pliers in the other hand, and pinch the tip of the wire in the nose of the pliers and coil the wire over (figure 5.18).
- Wind the wire down onto the base of the form until it is tight. You will feel the knot in the palm of your hand lock up onto the head of the form when the wire is secure (figure 5.19).
- You should feel no movement when you try to move the wire.

- Slip warp between thumb and forefinger of left hand.
- Draw the back wire firmly to the front using right hand.
- Switch the front wire across tightly (taking it underneath the wire you have brought to the front), taking it to the back (figure 5.26).

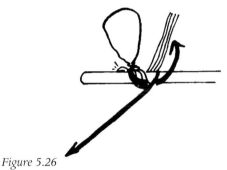

Figure 5.26

- Grip both wires tightly with right hand and pull down firmly as you push the dowel up to tighten the crossed wires at the top (figure 5.27).

Figure 5.27

- Repeat wrapping the thread, crossing and tightening the wires until sufficient ruff is made to wrap around the waist 2–3 times.
- Twist wires 3 times to fix end.
- Remove from dowel (figure 5.28).

To attach the ruff:
- The ruff goes around the waist 2 or 3 times.
- Position the looped end of wire against the head and wind around until the wires meet, once again making sure there is neither a gap nor overlap.

Figure 5.28

- Twist the two ends 5 or 6 times tightly.
- Cut excess wire and turn sharp ends over.

To trim the skirt:
sharp scissors
steam (boiling water in a saucepan)
wide-toothed comb

- Taking care not to scald anyone, twist the tassel over the steam so the kinks drop out. Comb, and hold it up at eye level to trim the uneven edges. Hang up to dry.

CHAPTER 6

Isis

The pompom tassel is made from wool. The finer the wool, the easier it is to make the balls fluffy. Weaving wool is particularly suited to this tassel. It is worth seeking out a woollen mill (see page 135 for shopping guide—buying in bulk is very economical). Simply warp your hanks to the thickness of the more expensively packaged small quantities.

A three-part simple twisted rope has been tied with a dividing knot.

The form has three separate sections, each covered in turn. The form is covered with gimp, using the basic method, as is the smaller one of the beads. The larger bead is covered with tapestry wool.

The pompom skirt is made up of two levels. The upper is twenty-four loops made from a long hank; the lower is twenty-four pompoms made separately then tied, one per loop.

REQUIREMENTS

8 skeins Appletons Crewel Wool no. 149
   (burgundy)
8 skeins Appletons Crewel Wool no. 928
   (blue/grey)
8 skeins Appletons Crewel Wool no. 103 (mauve)
2 skeins Appletons Tapestry Wool
   no. 149 (burgundy)
1 skein Appletons Tapestry Wool
   no. 103 (mauve)
1 skein Appletons Tapestry Wool
   no. 928 (blue/grey)
4.5 m (5 yards) Mokuba Gimp (burgundy)

wooden form no. 2
wooden bead no. 1
wooden bead no. 3
1 m (1 $\frac{1}{8}$ yards) hobby wire
12 cm (5 in) x 1.6 gauge aluminium wire

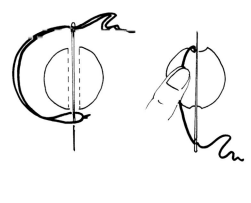

THE FORM

form
2 beads
3.5 m (3 $\frac{3}{4}$ yards) burgundy gimp for the form,
   1 m (1 $\frac{1}{8}$ yards) for the bead
other materials used to cover Nina tassel form
   (page 22)
wool needle
1.5 m (1 $\frac{2}{3}$ yards) burgundy tapestry wool
1 m (1 $\frac{1}{8}$ yards) blue/grey tapestry wool
6 m (6 $\frac{2}{3}$ yards) heavy linen thread (a dark colour)

Form no. 2 and bead no. 1
*   Cover the wooden form and one bead with
    gimp, using the method for Nina (page 22).

Bead no. 3
*   Thread a wool needle with 1.5 m (1 $\frac{2}{3}$ yards) of
    tapestry wool (burgundy). Cover the bead by
    wrapping the thread tightly around, through
    the hole in the centre and over the outside,
    until a neat cover is made (figure 6.1 a, b, c).
    Pass needle through the thread in the centre to

Figure 6.1a, b, c

fix the last wrap, then cut flush with the hole.
*   Thread the blue/grey and, using the same
    method, wrap over the top of the burgundy in
    bands to create stripes. Finish as with the
    burgundy.

THE SKIRT

To make the upper loops:
2 m (2 $\frac{1}{5}$ yards) warp x 4 ends tapestry wool
   (burgundy)
3 cm (1 $\frac{1}{8}$ in) template
1 m (1 $\frac{1}{8}$ yards) hobby wire
Nymo (000)

*   Use the Nina skirt technique (see page 23).
*   Wire 24 loops onto the template.
*   Do not cut the loops (figure 6.2). Make sure the
    beginning and end twists are really secure.
    Oversew both beginning and end neatly using
    fine thread such as Nymo to fix neatly. Then
    cut the hank close to the over-sewing.
*   Slide the loops from the template.

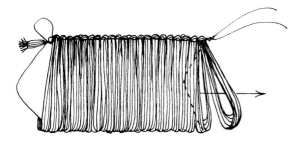

Figure 6.2

Work one colour at a time.

To make the pompoms:
8 hanks each of crewel wool, burgundy, blue/grey,
  mauve
dark linen thread
sharp scissors
2 chopsticks or pencils
carding comb, turkey brush or hard toothbrush
cup hot water

- Cut the linen thread into 24 x 25 cm (10 in) lengths.
- Remove labels and cut each skein of crewel wool and open flat to make hanks. Place 8 hanks together so you have 3 bundles: 3 blue/grey, 3 burgundy and 3 mauve.
- Cut 24 x 30 cm (12 in) lengths of linen thread. Soak 8 lengths of thread in hot water.
- Arrange in parallel lines spacing 3 cm (1 ⅛ in) apart. Place pompom hank on top (figure 6.3).

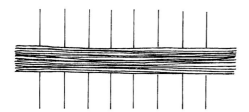

Figure 6.3

Figure 6.4a, b

- Tie the thread at even intervals along the hank, at first loosely, using a 'non slip' knot (figure 6.4). Check that the spacing is even.
- Proceed to tighten each one in turn by winding each of the ends of the linen thread around a chopstick to provide 'handles' enabling the threads to be pulled tightly without injuring your hands (figure 6.5).

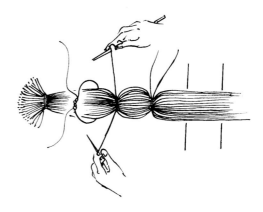

Figure 6.5

- Tie in turn along the hank to make 8 tightly tied bunches. Work back along the hank and tie a further 2 normal knots on top of the first non-slip knot (this equals 3 knots per bunch). The ends of each tie form a pair of securing threads.
- To check that each bunch is secure, squeeze tightly over the tie, and roll thumb and forefinger over each knotted area. If you feel the threads slipping and sliding under the knot, the ties are not tight enough.
- Repeat the process and tie the remaining 2 hanks.

To cut the pompoms:

- Use a sharp pair of scissors to cut between the ties (figure 6.6). To cut evenly around the hank, rotate the bunch as you cut and take care you do not snip the tying threads. You will have 24 tightly tied bundles of wool each having a pair of securing threads.

Figure 6.7

Figure 6.6

To shape the pompoms:

- Take a pompom by the securing threads and firmly squeeze between thumb and forefinger against the pile. Trim away the square edges and cut to a circular shape about the size of a 10-cent piece. Repeat, this time squeezing with the pile and trim the untidy edges to a circle.
- Hold the securing threads tightly, close to the pompom, and brush to make fluffy. Trim once more to make the round shape. The balls do not have to be perfect; often they seem a little flat on top where the tying thread is, but when they are attached to the skirt loops they take on a rounded appearance.
- Repeat this process until 24 pompoms have been completed.

To attach the pompoms:

- The skirt will fall into loops and may be defined if needed by separating the loops from the top with the eye of a needle (figure 6.7).
- Tie one pompom to each loop with three tight knots, at the bottom fold (figure 6.8 a, b).

Figure 6.8a, b

- Alternate the colours and trim the excess tying thread close to the pompom.

To attach the skirt:

- Treat the same as for Nina. Wind 2–3 times around the waist so wires meet and twist several times to secure.

THE ROPE

1.5 m (1⅔ yards) warp x 4 ends tapestry wool (each of the 3 colours)

- Make a 3-part rope (refer to rope making, page 16, and make this simple twisted rope).

THE DIVIDING KNOT

The dividing knot is seen most commonly on curtain tie-backs and it forms the two loops to go around the curtain.

- Hold up your rope and make an M (figure 6.9).

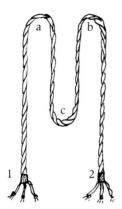

Figure 6.9

- Bring the 2 loops of the M together and place them flat over the palm of your left hand (figure 6.10).

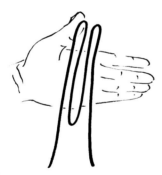

Figure 6.10

- Take outer free end and wind firmly underneath and along 3 or 4 times, towards the 2 loops (figure 6.11a, b).
- Flick the loose end down through loop **b** and wedge it between your index and middle fingers (figure 6.12).

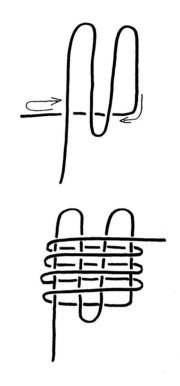

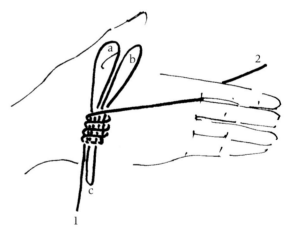

Figure 6.11a,b

Figure 6.12

- Pull one side of loop **c** to find which side will reduce loop **b** to lock the loose end in place (figure 6.13a, b).
- Adjust the remaining loops to make them even (figure 6.14).

To attach the rope:
The knot in this rope sits at the top of the form to keep the form segments locked together.

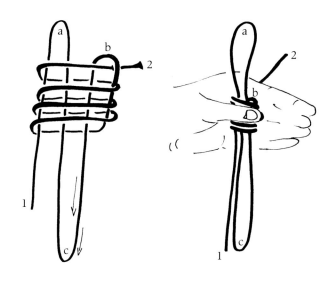

Figure 6.13a, b

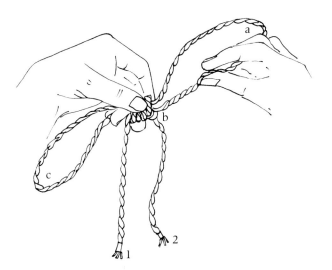

Figure 6.14

wool needle

40 cm (16 in) Nymo (D)

pliers

12 cm (5 in) x 1.6 gauge aluminium wire (bent at the tip of one end to a small, closed loop shape)

- Slip the loop of the wire into the coil of the dividing knot; pass the needle threaded with the linen thread in from the side of the knot (figure 6.15).

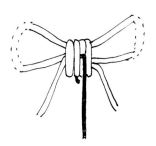

Figure 6.15

- Sew back and forth, each time taking the needle through the wire loop (you cannot see this but test it by pulling on the wire when the needle is pushed through the knot) (figure 6.16).

Figure 6.16

- Pull the two free ends of the rope together, down onto the wire and bind it tightly about 6 times, so the wire is sandwiched and bound firmly between the two rope ends close the knot (figure 6.17).
- Cut the two rope ends off close to the binding.

Figure 6.17

To attach the rope to the form:

- Thread the wire first onto the gimp bead, then the wool-covered bead and last the form.
- Hold the form segments in your hand with the knot in the palm, supporting them together. Pinch the tip of the wire between the tip of the pliers with the other hand. Coil the wire over to roll it down onto the base of the form, until you feel the knot lock up in the palm of your hand and the segments are secure (figure 6.18).

Figure 6.18

CHAPTER 7

Snow Queen

This is a large tassel and looks spectacular when made in pairs for curtain tiebacks.

As for the pompom tassel, the skirt has two parts: the upper section has forty-eight loops; the lower section consists of a mini tassel made onto each of the loops.

The form is covered with a plain gimp cover.

A thick velvet ruff is made for the waist. A smaller one covers the junction of the rope and form, and sits at each end of a dividing cylinder on the rope.

REQUIREMENTS

160 g (6 ½ oz) (6 ends coned) 1 ply Britt
    Mercerised Cotton no. 54 (off-white)
5 m (5 ½ yards) Mokuba Gimp (off-white)

wooden form no. 1
4 m (4 ½ yards) hobby wire
15 cm (6 in) 1.6 gauge aluminium wire

THE FORM

form
5 m (5 ½ yards) gimp
other materials as for Nina (see page 22).

- The form is covered in gimp using the same
  method as for Nina (see page 22)

THE SKIRT

To make the upper loops:
4.5 m (5 yards) warp x 6 ends (mercerised cotton
    warp ends x 10 times over a warping measure
    of 4.5 m/5 yards)
4.5 cm (1 ¾ in) template
1.75 m (2 yards) hobby wire
milliners needle
Nymo (D)

- Wire 48 skirt loops in the method for the Nina
  tassel skirt (page 23) but do not cut the loops.
  Oversew both the beginning and end of the
  skirt at the top edge with Nymo and cut the
  warp at the beginning and end close to the
  top, leaving no free ends.
- Slide the loops off the template and place flat
  on the table.

To make the mini tassels onto the loops:
1.8 m (2 yards) warp x 204 ends to make 16 mini
    tassels (warp 6 ends x 34 times over a warping
    measure of 1.8 m/2 yards) (there is a total of 48,
    so repeat twice using the same colour, or use
    three different colours)
wool needle
sharp scissors

matching thread (to bind necks of mini tassels)
4.5 cm (1 ¾ in) template with a fold

- Cut each mini tassel hank into 16 equal lengths
  by folding the hank in half, cutting, then repeating this to cut into quarters, eighths, and
  sixteenths until you have three groups of 16 x
  11 cm (4 ⅓ in) bundles. Cut and stack them
  (figure 7.1).

Figure 7.1

- One mini tassel is made onto each of the loops.
  (If using 3 different colours alternate the
  colours.)
- Attach one to each loop of the skirt. Once
  again as in the pompom skirt run the blunt
  end of a needle from the top to the base of each
  loop, if you have trouble defining the loops.
- Thread the first bundle through the loop and
  fold it onto itself so the ends are even.
- Thread a needle with 6 ends of Britt
  mercerised thread to wrap the necks of the
  mini tassels. Double and wet the end of the
  'wrap' to act as a 'brake' (the thread drags
  when the wet end is reached), eliminating the
  need for a knot.
- Hold the two hank ends firmly between the
  thumb and forefinger. Pass the needle through
  the hank from the right side just under the
  loop to bring it out in front.
- Wind the thread tightly around the neck four
  times (figure 7.2a), then sew through the binding so the needle passes through the neck to
  come out through the back (figure 7.2b). Snap
  the thread sharply and tightly, then cut the
  thread flush with binding.

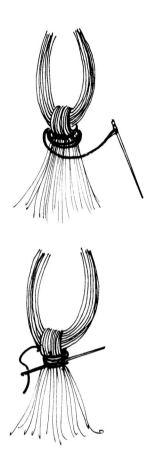

Figure 7.2a, b

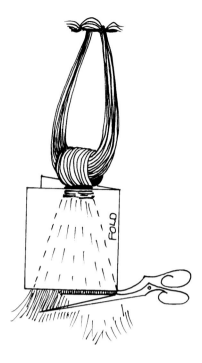

Figure 7.3

- Trim each of the 48 mini tassels separately. Lay the mini tassel on the template, and comb the threads smooth and flat. Fold the template around the mini tassel with its upper edge positioned just below the skirt loop. Hold firmly with thumb and forefinger and cut the threads hanging below the lower edge (figure 7.3). Cut from the outer edge to the centre; reverse to cut into the centre from the other side. This way the cut will be even.
- The skirt is attached by the same method as the Nina tassel. It will wind around the waist 3 or 4 times.

THE ROPE

The rope has a gimp-covered dividing cylinder. At each end of the cylinder a narrow wired ruff has been sewn in place to prevent the rope sliding about.

To make the rope:
3 x 2 m (2⅕ yards) warp x 60 ends mercerised
    cotton
other materials as for 3-part rope (page 16)

To make the cylinder:
4 cm (1⅔ in) length cut from used fax roll
1 m (1⅛ yards) gimp
adhesive

- Spray the cylinder with adhesive and cover with gimp (see Nina, page 22).

To assemble the rope:
15 cm (6 in) 1.6 gauge wire
pliers
needle
strong sewing thread

- Thread the rope through the cylinder. Slide the loops so they are equal.
- Attach the 1.6 gauge wire to the rope (see Nina, page 26).
- Thread wire through the top of the form, invert the tassel and use the pliers to lock the

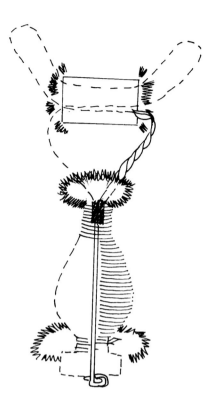

Figure 7.4

wire in place securely at the base of the form (figure 7.4).

THE RUFFS

To make the waist ruff:

2 m (2⅕ yards) warp x 150 ends mercerised cotton
    (warp 6 ends x 25 times)

2 pieces of fine corrugated cardboard, 3 cm x 2 cm
    (1⅛ in x ¾ in)

2 x 18 cm (7⅛ in) satay sticks

masking tape

sharp scissors

1.5 m (1⅔ yards) linen thread

- This ruff is rather like a pompom round the waist. The aim is to have a tight row of knots along the centre of the template.
- Set up the template by inserting two satay sticks into the corrugated cardboard 3 cm (1⅛ in) apart. Cut two small clips 1 cm (⅖ in) apart

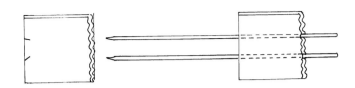

Figure 7.5

on the outer edge of one template (this is a left template) (figure 7.5).

- Thread linen thread between the satay sticks. Clip one thread through each notch and make thread ends even (figure 7.6).

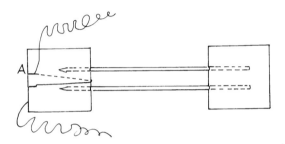

Figure 7.6

- Tape knotted end of warp to lower edge of left template—just below the stick.
- Wind the warp around the sticks once, going over the top and down the back.
- Release the thread from the clip at the back of the template. Bring it between the sticks to the front. Release the thread on the front of the template (figure 7.7). Tie a very tight non-slip knot in the centre of the warp. Drop one

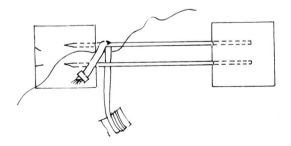

Figure 7.7

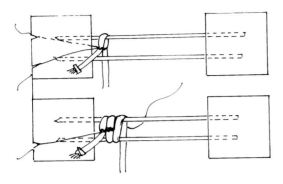

Figure 7.8

thread through the sticks, pull back tightly to lock at the back through clip. Lock the other thread tightly through the clip at the front (figure 7.8). Don't wind the warp tightly around the template, as it will pull apart and prevent the knots being pulled tight. Proceed in this manner until the template is filled.

- Remove adhesive tape from knot on the cardboard. Make sure knotting threads are free and dismantle template.

To attach the ruff:
30 cm (12 in) linen thread
chopsticks
rubber band

- The ruff when removed from the template naturally curls into a circle. Don't flatten or stretch it.
- Secure the skirt out of the way with a firm rubber band.
- Place the ruff around the waist of the form and push deep into the space with the tips of your fingers, working from the centre back to the front so the beginning and end butt together without a gap or an overlap.

- Thread one of the knotting threads onto a wool needle and sew through the beginning wrap of thread. Pull this thread gently to bring the beginning to butt with the end, to create a continuous band of ruff around the waist of the form (figure 7.9).

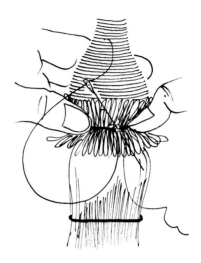

Figure 7.9

- Wet a 30 cm (12 in) length of linen thread, to pass as a 'belt' around the waist following the knots. Tie a non-slip knot, wind the ends around two chopsticks, then pull tightly to secure the ruff (figure 7.10). Tie off twice more. Cut the ends of the linen thread close to the knot.

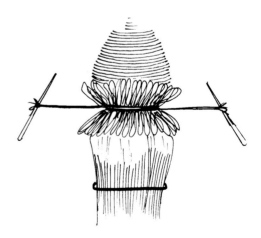

Figure 7.10

To clip the ruff:

The ruff is trimmed gradually, repeating the steps several times to create a neat velvety finish. The top and bottom edges may be trimmed to either a bevelled rounded shape or left longer and more square in appearance.

- Put a rubber band a few times around the skirt to hold it out of harm's way.
- Using sharp scissors cut the loops of the ruff. At this stage it will look 'wild and woolly', so don't be alarmed (figure 7.11).

Figure 7.11

- First hold the tassel in the position of viewing it from the top (have the knot pointing to your nose). Start to cut the centre outer edge, turning the tassel as you cut the untidy outer edges into a rounded shape (figure 7.12).

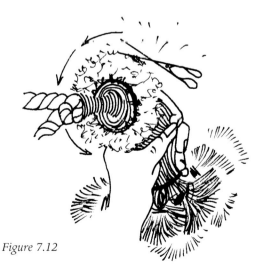

Figure 7.12

- Next, hold the tassel by the skirt and view from the side. Start to cut the top untidy edge into a line, once again turning the tassel with each cut (figure 7.13).

Figure 7.13

- Next grip the head of the tassel and start trimming the lower edge near the skirt, not forgetting to turn as you cut (figure 7.14).

Figure 7.14

- Repeat these steps until the ragged edges have been trimmed away and the ruff has a velvet finish.

To make the rope ruff:
1 m (1 ⅛ yards) x 36 ends mercerised cotton
    (6 ends together)
4 mm (⅛ in) dowel or knitting needle
75 cm (30 in) hobby wire

- See Nina, page 29, for the basic waist ruff and follow to the end of the method.
- Attach the rope ruff using a method similar to that of the skirt. The area where the rope enters the head may need to be padded out a little to provide a neat area to attach the ruff. It needs to be sewn in position to prevent the ruff separating and the wires showing, as well as to hold it in place. Use Nymo with a milliners needle and sew right into the rope segments to firmly secure.
- Clip loops and trim to a neat ball shape.

To make the cylinder ruffs:
2 x 0.5 m (½ yard) x 36 ends mercerised cotton
4 mm (⅛ in) dowel or knitting needle
2 x 75 cm (30 in) hobby wire
The method is the same as that used for the Nina waist ruff (page 29).

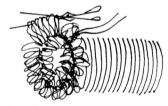

Figure 7.15

- Attach one ruff to each end flush with the ends of the cylinder and wire in place (figure 7.15).
- Use a long needle threaded with Nymo and sew the ruff to the rope to keep in place. Sew a few stitches right through the cylinder to secure one ruff to the other through the centre of the cylinder.

CHAPTER 8

Bohemia

This tassel looks very much like Snow Queen. It has the
same amount of thread and the basic pattern is the same.
However, the work in its making is about double.
I copied it from an old Italian tassel.

There is a cover of Perle 5 thread on the head of the form over
which a detached buttonhole stitch is worked.

A fine double cord suspends the mini tassels.

There is a thick velvet ruff at the top of the form and
another at the waist.

The thread is a mix of fine wool, chenille and mercerised
cottons in colours of aubergine, rust and avocado.

REQUIREMENTS

Taxtor Trading (wholesalers of bulk yarn, see suppliers, page 135) will supply the following 160 g (6 ½ ounces) total in the proportions given:

Avocado mixture

25 g (1 ounce) (Britt Mercerised Cotton no. 581 (avocado) (1 ply x 6 ends)

20 g (¾ ounce) Lauren Wool no. 928 (khaki) (1 ply x 6 ends)

18 m (19⅘ yards) chenille 3 ply (khaki) (3 ply x 1 end)

Rust mixture

25 g (1 ounce) Britt Mercerised Cotton no. 301 (burnt orange) (1 ply x 6 ends)

25 g (1 ounce) Lauren Wool x 2 each nos 916 (apricot), 926 (light brown), 831 (coral) (1.3 ply x 6 ends)

24 m (26⅖ yards) chenille 3 ply (khaki) (3 ply x 1 end)

Aubergine mixture

20 g (¾ ounce) Astor Machine Washable no. 867 (burgundy) (1.3 ply x 6 ends)

40 g (1 ½ ounces) Lauren Wool no. 918 (burgundy) (1.3 ply x 6 ends)

10 g (½ ounce) Lauren Wool no. 920 (blue) (1.3 ply x 1 end)

18 m (19⅘ yards) chenille 3 ply (aubergine)

6 m (6⅔ yards) chenille 3 ply (burgundy)

1 skein DMC Perle 5 no. 327 (aubergine)

2 skeins DMC Perle 5 no. 782 (rust)

wooden form no. 1

2.5 m (2¾ yards) hobby wire

15 cm (6 in) 1.6 gauge aluminium wire

THE FORM

form
1 hank DMC Perle 5 (aubergine)
other materials as for Nina (page 22)

Figure 8.1

- Follow the method for the Nina gimp-covered head, page 22, **spraying the head only once** (figure 8.1).
- Wind a band of thread around the waist of the covered form.

To decorate the head:
Detached buttonhole stitch (figure 8.2 detail) is a continuous buttonhole stitch worked over the

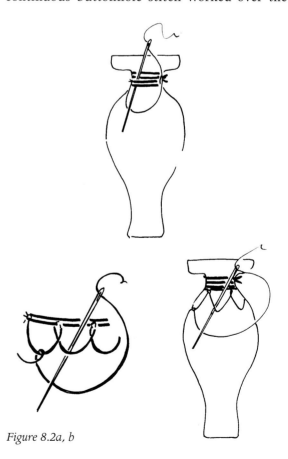

Figure 8.2a, b

surface to create a netting cover over all or part of the head. It is difficult to join thread in the middle of this stitch on a hard surface, so in estimating the quantity remember: **the more stitches you make in the first row, the longer the thread required to cover the head.** (I have worked only seven stitches on this one.)

2 m (2⅕ yards) DMC Perle 5 (rust)
wool needle
pencil or chopstick to fit snugly into the top of the form

- Hold the form upside down. Work a row of 7 loose buttonhole stitches evenly into the band of thread that has been wound around the waist of the form (figure 8.2a).
- Work the second row of stitches into the loops of the first row to start the mesh cover. Keep the stitching loose to allow for the increase in the diameter of the head (figure 8.2b).
- As the size of the head decreases allow for this by taking up the tension of your work to make the stitches smaller.
- When the head is four-fifths covered, set the pencil into the hole at the top of the form (the *bottom* of the inverted form). Pull the thread tight and wind it around the pencil 4 times (figure 8.3a).

Figure 8.3b

- Work the last row onto the thread around the pencil stretching the cover up as the stitches are made so the netting is neat and snug (figure 8.3b).
- Oversew into the band of thread several times to secure the thread before cutting it close to the work. Remove the pencil from the form.

THE SKIRT

To make the upper skirt:
Two 4.5 m (5 yards) cords need to be made before making the loops. It is the 3-part method which gives a finer quality cord.

3 x 5 m (5½ yards) warp x 6 ends Lauren wool
    (3 shades of rust mix) (1.3 ply x 6 ends), for
    one cord (repeat for second cord)
anchorage
cordless battery-operated drill, with a cup hook in
    the chuck
masking tape
weight

- Make one cord at a time.
- Use the first 3 warps to make a 3-part cord using a battery-operated drill in place of hand-twisting (see page 20).
- Secure one free end of each warp to anchorage.

Figure 8.3a

- Attach free end of first warp to cup hook on drill. Spin up until tight and ready to kink.
- Tape to floor and weight.
- Repeat to spin up remaining 2 warps to the same length as the first.
- Tape the 3 cords together and attach all 3 to the cup hook.
- Spin back together on reverse rotation.
- Repeat procedure to make a second cord.

To make the upper loops:
2 cords
2.5 cm (1 in) template
1.75 m (2 yards) hobby wire
milliners needle (no. 9)
Nymo (D)

- Make 48 loops as for Nina (page 23), wiring the two cords as you would a warped hank of thread (figure 8.4).

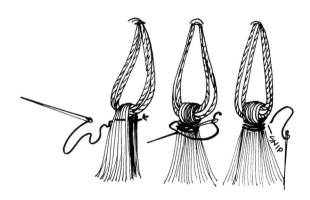

Figure 8.5a, b, c

- Make the mini tassels according to the instructions for Snow Queen (page 40), and attach one to each loop of cord, using the same method (figure 8.5a, b, c). Alternate the three colours.
- Trim each mini tassel in the same way (figure 8.6).

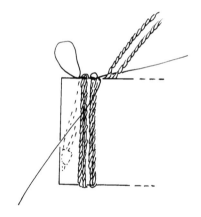

Figure 8.4

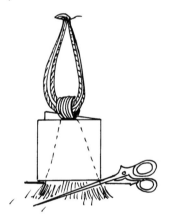

Figure 8.6

- Remove from the template.

To make the mini tassels onto the loops:
1.8 m (2 yards) warp x 100 ends to make 16 mini tassels (10 ends chenille, 50 mercerised cotton, 40 fine wool) in each colour mixture (rust, avocado, aubergine)
1 skein Perle 5 (rust) (to bind necks of mini tassels)
wool needle
sharp scissors

THE ROPE

2 m (2⅕ yards) warp x 18 ends mercerised cotton (burnt orange) (2 lengths)
2 m (2⅕ yards) warp x 18 ends mercerised cotton (avocado) (2 lengths)
1.75 m (2 yards) warp x 4 ends chenille (aubergine) (2 lengths)—chenille stretches when twisted so allow for this
1.75 m (2 yards) warp x 4 ends chenille (burgundy) (2 lengths)

- For equipment and basic method, see 4-part complex rope, page 18.
- For the first twist, the two rust sections are twisted up Z and plied back together S and taped.
- The two avocado sections are twisted up Z and plied back together S and taped.
- One maroon chenille is twisted Z with an avocado, plied S and taped.
- The second maroon and avocado are twisted Z and plied S and taped.
- For the second twist, the joined segments are now treated as you would make a simple rope.
- Anchor the four sections to a stable anchorage and in turn twist each segment further on the S twist until its fighting to twist back onto itself.
- Anchor and weight under tension as each one is twisted.
- Join the four and ply back to make a Z twisted rope.

To assemble the rope:
15 cm (6 in) 1.6 gauge aluminium wire
Refer to Nina, page 26, for instructions.

THE WAIST RUFF

2 m (2⅕ yards) warp x 72 ends Lauren wool aubergine mix (5 ends burgundy to 1 end blue)
2 pieces of fine corrugated cardboard, 3 cm x 2 cm (1⅛ in x ⅘ in)
2 x 18 cm (7½ in) satay sticks
masking tape
sharp scissors
1.5 m (1⅔ yards) linen thread

- Refer to Snow Queen, page 42, for the method used to make the waist ruff.

To attach the ruff:
30 cm (12 in) linen thread
chopsticks
rubber band

- Refer to Snow Queen, page 44, for the method used to attach and clip the waist ruff.

THE ROPE RUFF

1 m (1⅛ yards) warp x 30 ends Lauren wool combination burgundy, blue (5 to 1 as above)
4 mm (⅛ in) dowel or knitting needle
75 cm (30 in) hobby wire

- See page 30 for the Nina waist ruff and follow to the end of the method.
- Attach the rope ruff using a method similar to that of the waist ruff. The area where the rope enters the head may need to be padded out a little to provide a neat area to attach the ruff. It needs to be sewn in position to prevent the ruff separating and the wires showing, as well as to hold it in place. Use Nymo with a milliners needle and sew right into the rope segments to firmly secure.

CHAPTER 9

Esther

I made a version of this tassel for *World of Embroidery*, the English Embroiders Guild magazine. I chose it because it is 90 per cent Australian Angora from Littlewoods wool company of Benalla, Victoria. I bought huge hanks of the most beautiful variegated hand-dyed colours which I split and mixed, with no warping at all. It has a wonderful shine, feel and weight.

There are four parts to the form, each to be covered separately. The top and bottom sections are round shapes covered using the warped thread method. The middle two parts are a spindle shape and a 'squashed bead', each glued with a Perle thread covering.

The skirt is made up of two levels. The upper skirt consists of 30 loops onto which 30 puffballs or 'onions' are made. The puffballs are closely related to the mini tassels we made for

Snow Queen (page 39) and Bohemia (page 47). The techniques will be familiar.

The rope is double twisted and uses four colours. The rope is held at the top of the forms by a covered wire loop. The ends of the rope are bound together.

REQUIREMENTS

Appletons Crewel Wool
3 skeins no. 301 (acid gold)
2 skeins no. 101 (purple)
2 skeins no. 310 (acid green)

Appletons Tapestry Wool
2 skeins no. 301 (acid gold)
1 skein no. 101 (purple)
1 skein no. 895 (mauve/blue)
1 skein no. 451 (mauve)

Littlewoods hand-dyed Angora
1 x 75 g hank (3 ounces) no. 20 (mauve)
1 x 75 g hank (3 ounces) no. 4 (green)
1 x 75 g hank (3 ounces) no. 34 (purple)
1 x 75 g hank (3 ounces) no. 32 (acid gold)

2 skeins DMC Perle 5 no. 773 (acid green)
1 skein DMC Perle 5 no. 3047 (mustard)

wooden bead no. 5 (3.5 cm/1 $\frac{3}{8}$ in)
wooden form no. 4 (spindle shape)
wooden bead no. 2 (squashed shape)
wooden round form no. 10
small squashed bead
1.75 cm ($\frac{3}{4}$ in) hobby wire
20 cm (8 in) 1.6 gauge aluminium wire

THE FORM

To cover the round base:
round form no. 10
4 m (4$\frac{2}{5}$ yards) warp x 8 ends crewel wool (purple)
2 m (2$\frac{1}{5}$ yards) warp x 4 ends crewel wool
    (acid green)
2 posts (use warping board)
wool needle
1 m (1$\frac{1}{8}$ yards) Nymo (minimum)

- Secure one end of the purple warp securely to one post, and wind the warp around the two posts (figure 9.1). Work with the warp wound around the posts.

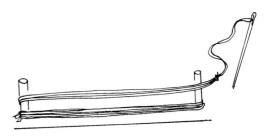

Figure 9.1

- Thread needle with linen thread, double and knot ends. Sew through warp end and fix the linen thread securely to it.
- Position the joined warp at the base of the round form with one hand, take the warp to the top and gently smooth the thread over the outside (figure 9.2).

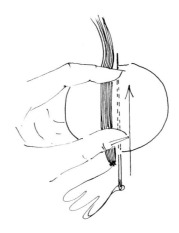

Figure 9.2

- Take the needle up through the centre hole, and hook it around the warp threads at the top (figure 9.3). Smooth warp down the outside.
- Pass the needle down through the hole and hook it around the warp threads at the bottom, maintaining the tension on the linen thread to keep the outside covering smooth and snug (figure 9.4).

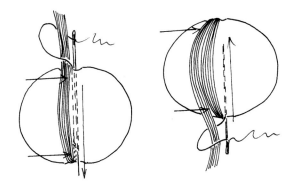

Figures 9.3, 9.4

- Flatten the warp covering with the needle to spread the thread and maintain a neat cover. Work in one direction around the form.
- As the warp is used release it gradually from the posts.
- Continue to cover the form using this method so the outside has a neat even cover of thread and the inside has only the fine linen thread holding the thicker outer covering firmly in place.
- Finish at base, by oversewing securely and running the needle through some of the centre thread. Cut warp and linen thread flush at the base.
- Repeat the above method with acid green to create even stripes around the form.

To cover the top ball:
bead no. 5
1 m (1⅛ yards) warp x 6 end crewel wool (purple)
1 m (1⅛ yards) warp x 6 end crewel wool (acid green)
wool needle
other materials as above

- Thread the wool needle with the acid green crewel wool and wrap the thread through the centre, covering the outside smoothly and evenly all around.

- Stripe over the top using the purple crewel wool.
- Finish by passing the needle through the centre, through a few threads, and cut flush with the bead.

To cover the spindle shape and squashed bead: These shapes are both covered horizontally using DMC Perle 5 thread.

Spindle
form no. 4
5 m (5½ yards) x Perle 5 (acid green)
other materials as for Nina form (page 22).

- Follow the method used to cover the form for Nina (page 22) **but spraying only once.**

Squashed bead
bead no. 2
3 m (3⅓ yards) x Perle 5 (mustard)
other materials as for Nina (page 22).

- Follow the method used for the spindle shape above.

The Skirt

To make the upper loops:
4 m (4⅖ yards) warp x 30 ends crewel wool (acid gold)
4.5 cm (1⅘ in) template
1.75 m (2 yards) hobby wire
Nymo (D)

- Wire 30 loops on the template, using the same method as for Nina (page 23). Do not cut the loops.
- Oversew both ends at the top edge with Nymo. Cut wool close to the wiring, leaving no tail.
- Slide loops off the template.

To make mini tassels:
300 g (12 ounces) Littlewoods Angora (75 g/ 3 ounces skein of each 4 colours)
wool needle
sharp scissors

1 hank Perle 5 (acid green) (binding thread for puffballs)

12.5 cm (5 in) template

- Cut each skein and open to make 1 x 1.8 m (2 yards) hank.
- Separate and mix colours to equal 3 warps x 80 ends. (This is equal to 100 ends of Appletons Crewel Wool.)
- In turn cut 10 x 12.5 cm (5 in) lengths from each warp.
- Thread one 12.5 cm (5 in) length through the first loop of the upper skirt. Fold in half onto itself and bind tightly with Perle thread close to the top (see Snow Queen, page 40).
- Repeat the process to make 30 mini tassels.

To make mini-tassels into puffball shapes:
- Bind a second binding about 2 cm (⅘ in) from the lower edge of each mini tassel (figure 9.5).

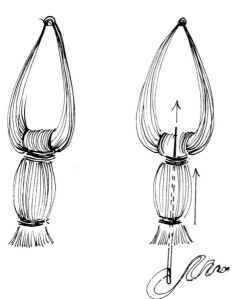

Figures 9.5, 9.6

- Thread a milliners needle with Perle binding thread. Double the thread and knot the ends with a tight neat knot. Pass the needle through the centre of the mini tassel from the bottom, and out through the top binding (figure 9.6). Pull sharply to create the onion shape. Wind

thread tightly once around the top binding. Take a small back stitch. Pass the needle back through the centre, bringing it out of the lower binding (figure 9.7a). Wind round once tightly, at the lower binding. Take a small back stitch in the binding (figure 9.7b).

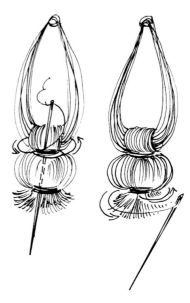

Figure 9.7a, b

- Sew through the binding again to come out through the top binding. Take a small back stitch, pull to tighten (figure 9.8) and cut flush with the top binding.

Figure 9.8

- Repeat this process, making an onion for each loop, and alternating the four colours.
- Trim the bottom edges to a round shape and brush with a carding comb or hard tooth brush to make the edges fluffy.

THE ROPE

The rope is double-twisted 4-part using 4 colours.

1 m (1⅛ yards) x 4 ends tapestry wool warps (acid gold) (4 warps)

1 m (1⅛ yards) x 4 ends tapestry wool (purple) (2 warps)

1 m (1⅛ yards) x 4 ends tapestry wool (mauve/blue) (1 warp)

1 m (1⅛ yards) x 4 ends tapestry wool (mauve) (1 warp)

- Anchor one end of each of the 4 pairs:
  —1 pair of acid gold
  —1 pair purple-mauve/blue
  —1 pair acid gold
  —1 pair purple-mauve
- Twist a 4-part complex rope following figures 4.16 to 4.19, page 18.

20 cm (8 in) x 1.6 gauge aluminium wire

1 m (1⅛ yards) x crewel wool (acid green)

wool needle

pliers

high impact adhesive

small squashed bead (2.5 cm/1 in)

- Bind the free ends of the rope firmly and neatly.
- Bind one end of the wire for 6 cm (2⅖ in) with the acid green crewel wool, and glue the wool in place at each of its ends with high impact adhesive.
- Place the rope over the covered end of the wire (figure 9.9a, b), and use pliers to turn a small closed loop in the wire. The rope is now attached to the wire.

To assemble form and attach skirt:
- Thread the smaller striped beads, spindle-

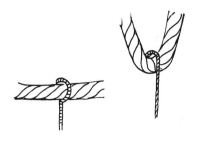

Figure 9.9a, b

shaped form, squashed bead and form no. 10 onto the wire in that order.

- The form has a hollow cavity at the base. Instead of the skirt being attached to the waist of the form it is housed inside this cavity. The finished skirt is wound around the centre wire which secures the rope to the form. Thread the squashed bead onto the wire and curl back with pliers to lock in place (figure 9.10).

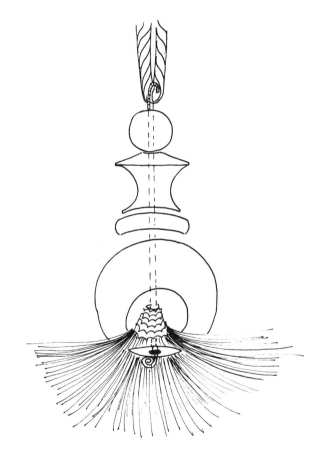

Figure 9.10

CHAPTER 10

Carmen

This tassel has a plain gimp-covered form.

The ruff has a ribbon base of 'leaves' to which five
velvet pansies are attached.

The basic skirt has an overskirt of bullion made from a very
long twisted skirt warp, or length of gimp. The skirt loops
remain uncut to twist back on themselves. The length
lost in spinning varies according to how tightly the
length has been spun and the thickness of the thread.
The finer the warp or gimp, the less the length
reduces. However, allow a reduction of
about ten per cent.

The rope is a simple three-segment rope with a
dividing knot sitting at the top of the form.

REQUIREMENTS

30 m (33 yards) Mokuba Gimp

1 reel each of YLI Pearl Crown Rayon no. 241
(scarlet), no. 285 (purple), no. 483 (fuchsia),
no. 800 (red)

1.5 m (1⅔ yards) x 1 cm (⅖ in) Mokuba Ribbon
no. 1512, no. 18 (green)

30 cm (12 in) x 9 mm (⅓ in) velvet ribbon (purple)

50 cm (19¾ in) x 9 mm (⅓ in) velvet ribbon
(fuchsia)

embroidery floss in contrasting pansy colours

15 seed beads in pansy colours

wooden form no. 1

2.5 m (2¾ yards) hobby wire

15 cm (6 in) 1.6 gauge aluminium wire

THE FORM

wooden form no. 1

5 m (5½ yards) gimp (red)

materials for a basic gimp-covered form (page 22).

- Follow the method for covering the form of
  Nina (page 22)

THE SKIRT

To make the underskirt:

7.5 m (8¼ yards) warp x 28 ends rayon thread
(pass all 4 colours over 7.5 m measure 7 times)

10 cm (4 in) template

masking tape

sharp scissors

- Follow the method for Nina (page 23).

To attach the underskirt:
- Follow the method used for Nina (page 28).

To make the overskirt:

25 m (27½ yards) gimp

11 cm (4⅖ in) template

battery-operated drill

stable anchor

masking tape

scissors

cardboard cylinder (such as a used cling wrap
cylinder)

1.5 m (1⅔ yards) hobby wire

- Keep everything you need within reach—your
  cardboard cylinder, scissors, tape and drill.
  Also cut tape ready for use.
- Secure the gimp on a stable anchor. Place scissors and cut pieces of masking tape close by.
  Anchor the other end of the gimp securely in
  the chuck of the drill. Hold taut and spin up
  the thread until it is wobbly and fighting hard
  against further twisting.
- Holding the tension, remove the twisted end
  from the drill and tape the ends securely to the
  cardboard cylinder. Maintaining tension, wind
  the twisted thread neatly onto the cylinder
  (figure 10.1). Secure the other end with tape
  after removing it from the anchor, without
  losing the twist at the end.

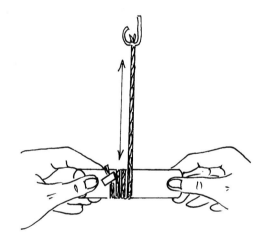

Figure 10.1

- Leave the twists to 'set' for at least a day for
  easier management.

To wire the overskirt:
- Wire the overskirt using the method for Nina
  (page 28). Be neat and even as you wind the
  thread around the board. Start the skirt by

attaching the wire to the end of the gimp without losing any of the twist.

- Finish securely with several twists of the wire.
- Slide each loop separately from the board and twist back to make the bullions. Bend the template and slide the work over close to its edge to make it easier to remove the loops (figure 10.2).

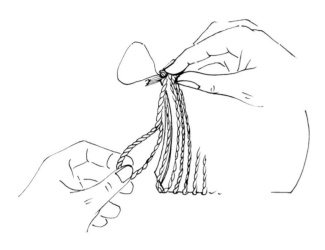

Figure 10.2

- Steam the skirt over a boiling saucepan of steam to set twists. Use kitchen tongs or oven mitts to prevent scalding your hands.

To attach the overskirt:
The skirt goes only once around the waist and is positioned above the underskirt on the waist of the form. Twist the two wire ends tightly together about 5 times, cut the wire close to the twist and turn the sharp ends in.

THE ROPE

1 m (1⅛ yards) warp x 15 ends rayon thread (red)
1 m (1⅛ yards) warp x 15 ends rayon thread
    (7 ends scarlet, 8 ends fuchsia)
1 m (1⅛ yards) warp x 15 ends rayon thread
    (purple)
15 cm (6 in) x 1.6 gauge aluminium wire

- Follow the method for a simple 3-part rope described on page 16.
- Make the dividing knot and attach the wire to the rope. (Refer to Isis, page 36, and follow instructions, omitting the two extra beads when assembling the rope with the form.

THE RUFF

1.5 m (1⅔ yards) Mokuba ribbon (green) (leaves)
pencil
1 m (1⅛ yards) hobby wire

- Fold the ribbon into 3, so there are 3 thicknesses to work with.
- Take wire and double it, and twist to form a loop at the folded end (figure 10.3a). Loop over about 1 cm (⅖ in) 'tail' of ribbon and twist to secure (figure 10.3b).
- Position attached ribbon and wire onto needle (figure 10.3c).
- The same method is used as for the Nina ruff (page 29).

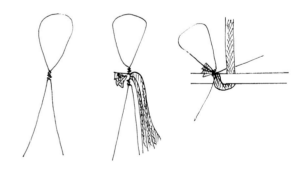

Figure 10.3a, b, c

To attach the ruff:
The ruff will wind once around the neck. Place in position and twist the starting loop of wire with the end ones to completely encircle the neck. Twist the wires 5 or 6 times, then cut ends. Bend the sharp edges over.

To make the pansies:

30 cm (12 in) 9 mm ($\frac{1}{3}$ in) velvet ribbon (back
petals)

50 cm (19 $\frac{3}{4}$ in) 9 mm ($\frac{1}{3}$ in) velvet ribbon of
contrasting colour (front petals)

number 9 milliners needle

Nymo (D)

Fray Stopper (or hair spray)

embroidery floss

seed beads

- The 5 pansies are made from velvet ribbon. Cotton velvet is best but is hard to come by. The 100 per cent polyamide works well, especially if washed and crushed. Double-sided is best, but single-sided will do.
- For the back petals, cut 30 cm (12 in) ribbon into 10 equal lengths (3 cm/1 $\frac{1}{8}$ in). Spray each end with Fray Stopper.
- Overlap 2 lengths at right angles (right sides together if ribbon is single-sided) and pin across.
- Thread a single thread of Nymo. Make a secure knot at the free end. Anchor the first stitch securely at a). Oversew this stitch once to make sure it is anchored permanently. Make large, even running stitches to point b) (figure 10.4). Do not let them overlap otherwise it will be difficult to gather your ribbon.

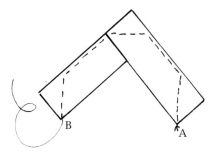

Figure 10.4

- Hold in shape with your left hand to prevent the ribbon twisting and pull tightly to make rounded shape (figure 10.5). Pinch tightly to gather and sew a tight back stitch to secure.

back petals

Figure 10.5

Buttonhole stitch tightly along the bottom edge at c).

- For the front petals, cut the 50 cm (20 in) ribbon into 5 x 10 cm (4 in) lengths. Fold the ribbon into thirds. Secure the folds with pins (figure 10.6).

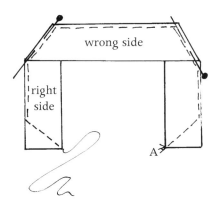

Figure 10.6

- Make a gathering thread as shown using Nymo. Secure the first end firmly at a). Stitch following the pattern as shown in figure 10.6.
- Remove pins and hold in place with your left hand. Draw stitching together to gather the lower petals into shape. Pinch firmly with the left hand to hold gathers and back stitch last stitch to secure gathering (figure 10.7).
- Fold lower petals in half, lengthways, so that the edges d) and e) meet. Oversew the raw edges d) and e) to hold them together (figure 10.8).
- Open the pansy. Pull the free end of the Nymo to double the thread and sew through the lower petal and over the top to close the hole in the pansy's centre. Repeat a few times,

REQUIREMENTS

1 spool each of YLI Pearl Crown Rayon no. 40
(natural), no. 103 (peach), no. 772 (gold)

100 g (4 ounces) Britt Mercerised Cotton no. 618
(pale gold), no. 54 (ecru), no. 680 (pale
green)—2 ends of each colour mixed (see
Taxtor Trading, page 136)

3 spirals Madeira Embroidery Floss Mouliné
no. 1111 (pale aqua)

11.5 m (12⅔ yards) Mokuba Gimp no. 15 (gold)

1.5 m (1⅔ yards) x 7 mm (¼ in) Mokuba
Embroidery Ribbon ES1540 no. 374 (green)

20 cm (8 in) x 7 mm (¼ in) each of Mokuba
Embroidery Ribbon ES1540 no. 002 (pale
pink), no. 034 (rose pink), no. 198 (lavender),
no. 514 (pale aqua), no. 214 (powder blue),
no. 287 (grey blue), no. 470 (cream), no. 429
(daffodil)

180 cm (2 yards) linen thread

packet seed beads, mixed pastel colours

wooden form no. 1
wooden bead no. 8
wooden bead no. 4
1 m (1⅛ yards) hobby wire
16 cm (6⅖ in) 1.6 gauge aluminium wire

THE FORM AND ROPE BEAD

To cover the form and beads:
gimp (gold)
form
bead no. 4
bead no. 8 (rope bead)

- Follow the instructions for covering the form
  in Nina (page 22).
- The form and bead no. 4 are later joined with
  wire (see page 69) and bead no. 8 is attached to
  the rope (see page 69).

THE SKIRT

To make the underskirt:

9 m (10 yards) warp x 21 ends rayon thread
(natural, peach, gold)

9 m (10 yards) warp x 18 ends mercerised cotton
(colours as given)

- Follow Nina instructions to make the skirt
  (page 23). Attach the skirt to the covered form
  (page 28).

To make the trellised overskirt:

21 ends of following mix

1.8 m (2 yards) warp x 3 ends embroidery floss
(pale aqua)

1.8 m (2 yards) warp x 6 ends rayon thread
(natural, peach, gold)

1.8 m (2 yards) warp x 12 ends mercerised cotton
(colours as given)

linen tying thread

wool needle

sharp scissors

matching thread to bind trellising

- The overskirt is made up of separate hanks,
  tied individually to the thread at the neck of
  the form, then divided and plaited to give a
  trellised pattern.
- Cut 6 x 20 cm (8 in) lengths of linen thread.
  Cut the warps into 6 x 30 cm (12 in) hanks.
  Fold each of the 6 trellis warps in half and loop
  one linen thread onto each at the fold, so the
  ends are about equal (figure 11.1).

Figure 11.1

- It is easier if you place the tassel onto a post for a comfortable working position.
- Tie the first hank tightly to the waist with the linen thread. Tie 2 more knots to safely secure, then cut the linen thread close to the knot.
- Tie a further 2 hanks, evenly spaced one third apart. The remaining 3 are tied between the spaces, making a total of 6 pairs evenly spaced around the waist, each tied with 3 tight knots (figure 11.2).

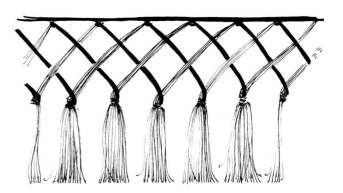

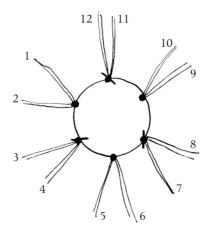

Figure 11.2

- To trellis cross the second group of threads from the first hank over the first group from the second (figure 11.3).

Figure 11.3

- Work 2 or more rows in this manner before binding two groups together neatly at an 'X' to keep from unravelling (figure 11.4).

Figure 11.4

THE ROPE

1 m (1 ⅛ yards) warp x 10 ends rayon thread (4 segments) (gold)

1 m (1 ⅛ yards) warp x 10 ends rayon thread (2 segments) (peach)

1 m (1 ⅛ yards) warp x 10 ends embroidery floss (2 segments) (aqua)

winding device

anchor

masking tape

- The rope is double twisted to become a complex rope.
- See 4-part double-twisted rope, using mixed colours, example A (page 18).

To assemble the rope and tassel:

rope

covered form

covered bead no. 4

covered bead no. 8

wool needle

linen or some strong thread

16 cm (6⅖ in) 1.6 gauge aluminium wire

pliers

scissors

- Only one rope enters the head.

- Use pliers to turn a small closed loop at one end of the wire. Fit the loop into the body of the rope.
- Thread the needle, double the thread and knot the end neatly. Pass the needle back and forth through the rope, pulling down on the wire to make sure the thread has passed through the wire loop.
- Bind the thread tightly around the base of the hook 5 times, then sew through the binding, pull tightly to lock the stitch and cut the thread flush with the rope. Cut the end off the rope flush with the binding.
- Thread wire through bead no. 4, then covered form.
- Use pliers to twist the end of the wire to lock at the base of the form.
- Bind the free end of the rope tightly with strong thread and trim close to the binding.
- Thread the end of the rope through the large covered bead twice and knot the end with a simple overhand knot to hide the binding.

THE RUFF

To make the ruff:
1.5 m (1⅔ yards) embroidery ribbon (green)
1 m (1⅛ yards) hobby wire
pencil

- The ruff base is made with ribbon as a base for the flowers.
- Double the wire and twist a loop in the end. Fold the ribbon into thirds and attach to the wire (figure 11.5).
- Follow the same method as for the Nina tassel ruff (page 29), substituting ribbon for thread. Make enough to fit once only around the waist.

To attach the ruff:
The ruff is placed around the waist and the wires twisted together tightly to secure. The ends are then

Figure 11.5

cut close to the twist. Turn the sharp edge in with pliers.

Floral Embellishment
20 cm (8 in) x 7 mm (¼ in) embroidery ribbon in each of colours given
1 m (1⅛ yards) hobby wire
embroidery floss (green)
Nymo (00)
seed beads in variety of soft colours
hair spray
cotton thread to cover join
milliners needle (no. 9)

The silk and bead flowers are made separately and then attached. For most of the silk flowers I have taken inspiration from *The Artful Ribbon* by Candice Kling. She works mostly with wide wired ribbon and attaches it to crinoline but her designs adapt well to making much smaller flowers.

You can make whatever flowers you wish and substitute any ribbon. Because this ribbon is so fine I use it double. As well, using two colours together gives some depth of shade.

To make the 5-petal flowers:
- Cut 2 lengths of ribbon about 10 cm (4 in) long,

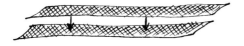

Figure 11.6

and place one on the other (figure 11.6). Thread the needle with about 30 cm (12 in) of Nymo (00) double and knot the end tightly.

- Work a running stitch to make the petals (figure 11.7).

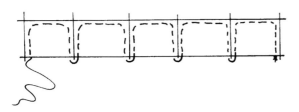

Figure 11.7

- Spray the ribbon with hair spray to wet it, and pull up gently to gather it into the little petal shape. Butt the two raw edges together and oversew to close the circle (figure 11.8). Sew a small seed bead in the centre.

Figure 11.8

- Attach the flowers to the ruff by sewing firmly, between the leaves, onto the wire base.

To make a daffodil:
- Use cream ribbon as the saucer and follow the above method.
- The cup is made with about 7 cm (2 ⁴/₅ in) of double ribbon. Use a running stitch worked along the bottom edge (figure 11.9). Spray,

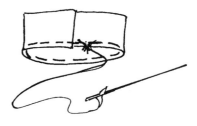

Figure 11.9

gather and oversew the gathered area. The 'cup' is then sewn through the middle onto the saucer, and there is the daffodil (figure 11.10). It is then sewn onto the wired area on the ruff to join the bunch.

To make the seed bead flowers:
- These are really easy. Take about 10 cm (4 in) wire and thread on 7 seed beads (figure 11.11). Take one end of the wire and re-thread at least

Figure 11.10

Figure 11.11

Figure 11.12

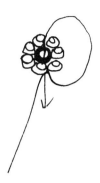

Figure 11.13b

the first 3 beads (figure 11.12). Pull up tight into a circle. Thread on the centre bead (this one should be a tiny bit larger) (figure 11.13a). Thread the wire down through the centre of the circle of beads, and pull tight to lock the centre in place in the middle (figure 11.13b). Twist the two wires together (figure 11.13c).

- Thread the milliners needle with about 30 cm (12 in) green embroidery floss. Double, knot tightly and neatly, trim the tail close to the knot. Sew up through the centre of the flower and back through the tail of the thread. When the thread is pulled tight it is locked by the

Figure 11.13c

knot. Start to wind the thread around the wire close to the beads. When a little wire is covered and your fingers fit you can spin the wire to cover the remaining wire quickly. If you can't do this just keep winding the thread round and round till the wire is covered. Sew back into the last few wraps of binding to secure, then cut thread.

To attach the flowers:
- Attach all the flowers to the ruff wire by sewing with Nymo. Curl the leftover covered wire of the seed bead flowers into loops to look like leaves.
- I have sewn little bunches of beads and wire leaves to the trellis binding, and also as another ruff where the ball sits at the head (figure

Figure 11.13a

REQUIREMENTS

1 reel YLI Pearl Crown Rayon no. 899 (bright
    turquoise)
100 g (4 ounces) x 6 ends Britt Mercerised Cotton
    no. 303 (turquoise) and no. 792 (peacock)
3 Spirals Madeira Embroidery Floss Mouline no.
    706 (fuchsia)

wooden form no. 5
3.5 m (3⅘ yards) hobby wire
15 cm (6 in) 1.6 gauge aluminium wire

THE FORM

To make chevron cords:
4 m (4⅖ yards) warp x 6 ends mercerised cotton
    (mix of turquoise and peacock) x 2 for S twist
    cord
repeat for 4 m (4⅖ yards) Z twist cord
winding device
anchor
masking tape
high impact glue
other materials to cover Nina form (page 22)

* Refer to instructions for making S and Z cords
  (page 14).
* Glue each end of both the cords with a high
  impact glue, and when dry cut the ends so
  they are neat and secure.

To cover the form:
* Spray the form with glue, first using the basic
  directions to prepare for spraying (page 22).
* First place one cord and bond it with the top of
  the form, then take one turn to start covering
  the top (figure 12.1). Just before you complete
  the turn attach the other cord to butt against
  the first (figure 12.2).
* Start the second row with the new cord and
  complete one turn.
* Now the pair can be used as one (keeping them
  flat against each other). Be sure no wood is
  visible beneath (figure 12.3).

Figure 12.1

Figure 12.2

* Cut the ends when the cover is complete.

To cover the metal strips:
4 x 3 mm (⅛ in) strips from an aluminium can
    (5 mm/¹⁄₁₀ in longer than head of form)

Figure 12.3

Figure 12.4

1 spiral embroidery floss (fuchsia)
high impact glue
spray adhesive
all-purpose scissors
tape measure
felt-tipped pen

- Spray the strips of aluminium lightly with spray adhesive, and let it become 'high tack'.
- Bond the end of the embroidery floss onto the metal strip and wind the thread carefully and neatly to cover the strip from one end to the other, so no metal is visible beneath.
- Lightly run a thin line of glue on one side of the strip, and let it become tacky.
- Space and attach the strips at four even intervals around the head of the form. Divide into four and mark if your eye is not good.
- Bend the metal at the top and base to make edges neat.
- Glue an S and a Z cord either side of each of the strips to form a chevron pattern. Make sure

the ends have a dab of glue to prevent the thread ends unravelling (figure 12.4).

THE SKIRTS

To make the underskirt:
9 m (10 yards) warp x 42 ends, 1 rayon thread (bright turquoise), 6 mercerised cotton (peacock, turquoise), warped 6 times (6 ends rayon, 36 ends mercerised cotton)
13 cm (5 ¼ in) template
1.5 m (1 ⅔ yards) hobby wire
masking tape

- Follow basic skirt method for the Nina tassel (page 23).
- Attach the underskirt according to the Nina skirt method (page 23).

To make the overskirt:
10 m (11 yards) warp x 14 ends, 1 rayon thread (bright turquoise), 6 mercerised cotton (turquoise and peacock), warped 2 times

(2 ends rayon, 12 ends mercerised cotton)
winding device (battery-operated drill)
cylinder or card to hold wound thread
masking tape
scissors
14.5 cm (5⅘ in) template

- The overskirt is a long twisted warp of thread
  that is twisted up on a drill then wrapped on
  the template and wired. The loops spring back
  on themselves when removed from the board
  to become small cords.
- Anchor one end of the 10 m (11 yards) warp
  and spin up until it is ready to spring back
  onto itself.
- Remove from the anchor, maintaining the
  tension, and wind onto a holding cylinder or
  card. Tape the end to secure.
- Make the skirt following the directions for
  making the Nina skirt (page 23).
- However, to start, attach the wire securely to
  the end of the warp without leaving a tail.
  Keep the twisted yarn taut at all times.
- Slide the loops carefully along the template to
  remove the skirt from the board, one loop at a
  time. Let each cord loop twist back onto itself
  as it is released.

To attach the overskirt:
The overskirt sits over the underskirt and wraps
once only. Twist the beginning loop of wire tightly
to the end wires and cut the ends close to the twist.
Bend the sharp edges under.

THE ROPE

1 m (1⅛ yards) warp x 24 ends mercerised
    cotton (turquoise and peacock) x 6 times
winding device (chopstick or pencil)
anchor
cardboard cylinder
masking tape

- Use the method for a 3-part double-twisted
  rope (page 17).

THE DIVIDING KNOT

The dividing knot forms the two loops to go around
the curtain.

- Refer to Isis, page 36, for the method followed
  to form this knot.

To attach the rope:
wool needle
40 cm (16 in) linen thread
pliers
15 cm (6 in) 1.6 gauge aluminium wire, bent at the
    tip of one end to a small closed loop shape

- Refer to Isis (page 36) but when assembling
  note that you omit the beads and pass the wire
  directly through the wooden form.

THE RUFFS

To make and attach the waist ruff:
2 m (2⅕ yards) warp x 8 ends embroidery floss
    (fuchsia)
6 mm (¼ in) dowel
1 m (1⅛ yards) hobby wire
sharp scissors

- Make and attach the ruff following the Nina
  tassel ruff (page 29). Cut the ruff loops and
  trim to a neat finish using fine sharp scissors.

To make and attach the rope ruff:
1 m (1⅛ yards) warp x 6 ends embroidery floss
    (fuchsia)
4 mm (⅕ in) dowel
1 m (1⅛ yards) hobby wire
Nymo (D)
milliners needle
sharp scissors

- Make the rope ruff using the same method as
  for the waist ruff.
- Attach the rope ruff using a method similar to
  that of the waist ruff. The area where the rope

enters the head may need to be padded out a little as at the waist to provide a neat area to attach the ruff. It needs to be sewn in position to prevent the ruff separating and the wires showing, as well as to hold it in place.

- Use Nymo and a milliners needle and sew right into the rope segments to firmly secure.

CHAPTER 13

Diane de Poiters

The wooden form is first covered with dacron then pellan to
give a soft padded surface. A ribbon cover is bandaged over
the top and is oversewn with sprays of wisteria and
forget-me-nots held together by three bows and trails.
There is a gilded lozenge-shape bead at the top of
the head and a ribbon-covered bead sits above.

The skirt is simple.

The ruff is made from spun-thread covered wire flowers
alternating with gold-covered beads.

The rope is a simple three-part rope with a covered dividing
cylinder, padded and embellished in the same way as the
head of the form, to separate the loops on the rope.

Requirements

1 x 100 m (110 yards) reel YLI Pearl Crown Rayon
  in each of no. 103 (peach), no. 319 (green),
  no. 432 (grey/blue), no. 772 (gold)
1 spiral Madeira Metallic Thread no. 5015 (gold)
1 reel fine Madeira Metallic Sewing Thread no. 6
  (gold)
selection of embroidery floss in pastel colours
2.5 m (2¾ yards) embroidery floss (blue)
5 m (5½ yards) x 8 mm (⅓ in) Mokuba
  Embroidery Ribbon no. 1512 (gold)
20 cm (8 in) x 7 mm (¼ in) Mokuba Embroidery
  Ribbon in each of no. 347 (green), no. 470
  (cream)
1 m (1⅛ yards) x 7 mm (¼ in) Mokuba
  Embroidery Ribbon no. 241 (blue)
10 cm (4 in) x 90 cm (36 in) dacron
10 cm (4 in) x 90 cm (36 in) pellan

wooden form no. 1
wooden bead no. 2
wooden squashed bead no. 2
1 sheet Schlag Dutch metal film
3 m (3⅓ yards) hobby wire
16 cm (6⅖ in) 1.6 gauge aluminium wire

The Form

To cover the form:
form
dacron padding
pellan
4 m (4⅖ yards) gold embroidery ribbon
Nymo (D)
1.5 m (1⅔ yards) Perle 5
milliners needle

- Follow the Nina method to spray the form
  (page 22).
- Cover the head with a single layer of the
  dacron, coiling it neatly from top to bottom
  (figure 13.1).
- Cover again, using 1.5 cm (⅔ in) pellan strips,
  starting again at the top, but using no glue.

Figure 13.1

This time leave about a 3 mm (⅛ in) cuff above
the form. Wind firmly, covering the surface
about three times by making a figure of eight
pattern until the form is evenly covered.
Secure any ends with a needle and thread,
using no knots (figure 13.2a).

Figure 13.2a

Figure 13.2b

- Sew a running stitch around the cuff edge at the top and pull in to make a neat covered edge. Oversew to secure thread (figure 13.2b).
- Repeat covering, using the gold ribbon to completely and evenly cover the form (figure 13.3).

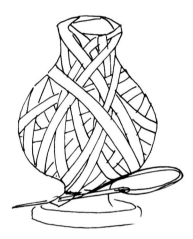

Figure 13.3

- Wind a band of Perle 5 around the waist to provide a base for attaching the flower and bead ruff.

To gild squashed bead:
bead
1 sheet Schlag Dutch metal film
chopstick
adhesive spray
water-based sealer (high gloss)
cotton gloves
soft brush

- Sit bead on chopstick and spray lightly with adhesive.

- Wearing gloves, gently apply the sheet of metal over the high tack surface. Press gently to bond and lightly brush off excess with the brush.
- Use the brush to seal the gilding with one coat of water-based sealer.

To cover bead no. 2
25 cm (10 in) blue embroidery ribbon
25 cm (10 in) gold embroidery ribbon
50 cm (20 in) gold embroidery floss
wool needle
Nymo (D)
milliners needle

- Thread the first ribbon onto the wool needle and wrap through the centre of the bead, holding the tail so it will not pull through (figure 13.4).

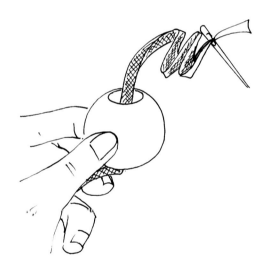

Figure 13.4

- Wrap the ribbon over the outside and through the centre, evenly spacing around the bead. Remove the needle and thread the other ribbon (figure 13.5).
- Hold the free end with your thumb and start to cover the gaps with the new ribbon. Sew the free beginnings and ends with the Nymo and

Figure 13.5

tuck any untidy ends into the centre of the bead.

- Thread needle with embroidery floss and sew through the centre hole to anchor. Border each ribbon edge with a wrap of the embroidery floss. Sew the last wrap through the centre to secure. Cut thread flush with the hole in the bead.

EMBELLISHMENTS

To make the ribbon bows:
20 cm (8 in) x 7 mm ($\frac{1}{4}$ in) embroidery ribbon in blue, cream, green
Nymo
pins
embroidery needles
gold metallic embroidery thread
gold metallic sewing thread

- Tie three ribbon bows with each 20 cm (8 in) length of ribbon.
- Pin and tack the first bow in position. Start by pinning the centre and then the trails in place. Tack in position, then secure the loops over the top.
- Repeat with the second and third bows, spacing them evenly around the head of the form.
- When the bows are fixed, couch thick gold thread over the top, following the edges of the ribbon (see glossary) (figure 13.6). Use the metallic sewing thread to couch. Be careful not to couch folds in the ribbon as this spoils the image.

Figure 13.6

To make the wisteria:
embroidery floss—2 shades of mauve, 3 shades of green
embroidery needles
chenille needle no. 9

- Use a combination of mauves to sew the wisteria petals. The upper petals are solid colour and the lower are mixed mauves to give light and shade. The sprays are worked from the outside in as it is much easier to create movement in your work this way. The petals are worked loosely in a V shape starting from the top. When the V is complete, a long stitch closes the centre. The leaves and stems are worked using some solid colours and some mixed to prevent a flat look.
- Start at the outer edge of the spray, working the petals first. Thread chenille needle (no knot). Bring needle through so the thread just disappears into the ribbon and make a french knot.
- Bring needle through to where the top of the first V shape is to be made. Pass the needle through the base at b) and up to the opposite side to bring the needle out at c) (figure 13.7).

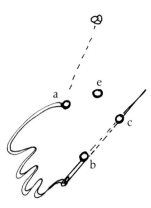

Figure 13.7

- Pass needle through d) bringing it out at e) (figure 13.8).

Figure 13.8

- Pass needle through base at f) bringing it out at the point you will start the next V shape making the new a) (figure 13.9).

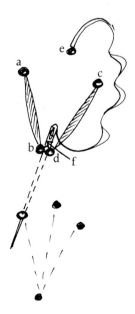

Figure 13.9

- Each spray needs to have its leaves, calyx and stems. Use two strands of green. The small flowers have only one leaf, a simple elongated lazy-daisy (see glossary). On the larger petals work two leaves.
- Bring the needle through the base (figure 13.10).

Figure 13.10

- Take needle through leaves and petals from right to left. Repeat 2 to 3 times to bind the base tightly (figure 13.11a).

Figure 13.11a

- Pass needle up through binding. Don't pull thread through all the way, leave a loop (figure 13.11b).
- Take needle through the back of the loop and pull down firmly leaving a long stitch to make the stem (figure 13.11c).
- Make a long couched stitch to make the stem, couching it into a curved shape.

Figure 13.11b

Figure 13.11c

- Follow the diagram of the bow and sprays of flowers or make up your own design (figure 13.12).

To make the forget-me-nots:
chenille needle no. 9
embroidery floss in 2 shades of blue
embroidery floss, yellow

- Random sprays of forget-me-nots are used to fill gaps on the ribboned surface.
- Work 5 french knots in a circular pattern (see glossary).
- A yellow sixth french knot is worked in the centre of the circle of blue.
- Leaves are worked in lazy-daisy stitch in green (see glossary).
- Green stems are couched in curved patterns.

THE SKIRT

9 m (10 yards) warp x 30 ends rayon thread (peach, green, grey/blue, gold) (the 4 colours are warped 9 m/10 yards x 7 times giving 28 ends: the green is warped twice more to make 30 ends in total)
13 cm (5 $\frac{1}{5}$ in) template
1.5 m (1 $\frac{2}{3}$ yards) hobby wire

- Make and attach the underskirt following the instructions used for Nina tassel (page 28).

Figure 13.12

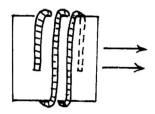

Figure 13.16

- Glue over the mark and let dry. Then cut in the centre of the glue. The open length of wire is the size all the flowers will be.
- Use this short wire to mark along the full length of the covered wire with the pen, then place a drop of glue at each mark, let dry, and cut through the centre of each glued area.
- In turn, wind each length onto the template, slide off and keeping the shape, sew the centres with a double thread of Nymo. Bind over tightly about five times then catch through the binding to secure (figure 13.17). Cut flush with wire.

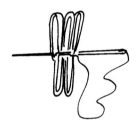

Figure 13.17

- Thread needle with contrasting embroidery floss and bind over the top of the Nymo to finish the centre.
- Bend to shape with a pair of fine pliers (figure 13.18).

Figure 13.18

To attach the flowers:

Arrange the beads at even intervals around the waist. Sew the wire flowers in between the bead spaces, the last one locking them all securely in place (figure 13.19).

Figure 13.19

CHAPTER 14

Coppelia

The form of this tassel is ceramic and hollow so the skirt fits
inside and sits locked by a button at the base of the rope.
A wooden form could be used to recreate
something like this.

The simple basic underskirt has an overskirt made up of a series
of twelve wooden pendant drops. The wooden beads are first
sealed then painted and sealed with varnish.

REQUIREMENTS

1 reel YLI Crown Pearl Rayon no. 771 (gold)

1 reel YLI Crown Pearl Rayon no. 772 (gold)

1 spiral Madeira Mouline no. 1414 (lime)

1 spiral Madeira Mouline no. 1610 (acid gold)

1 spiral Madeira Mouline no. 0612 (pink)

2 hanks each of DMC Perle 5, no. 3688 (pink) no. 427 (green)

ceramic form—hollow

wooden beads (see templates, page 9)

Jo Sonja Acrylic paints—suggested colours: white, cadmium yellow medium, dioxine purple, ultramarine deep blue, cobalt blue, turquoise, napthol crimson, green oxide, orange, magenta

1.5 m (1⅔ yards) hobby wire

gesso

high gloss varnish

THE SKIRT

To make the underskirt:

7.5 m (8¼ yards) warp x 24 ends rayon thread, 12 ends of each shade of gold

7.5 m warp x 1 end Mouline (lime)

7.5 m warp x 1 end Mouline (acid gold)

14 cm (5⅔ in) template

1.5 m (1⅔ yards) hobby wire

- Make the skirt following the instructions for Nina (page 23). (The skirt is not attached until the rope is complete.)

To make the overskirt:

(make 12 cords of each colour; for each cord)

30 cm (12 in) x 1 end Mouline (lime)

30 cm (12 in) x 1 end Mouline (pink)

stable anchor

tape

winding device

scissors

- Pair the threads, one of each colour.
- Double one, knot the end and loop the knot

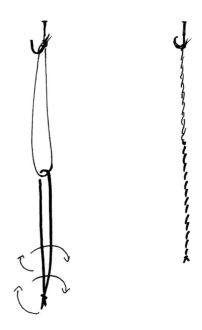

Figure 14.1a, b

end over the anchor. Thread the second colour through the first and knot the free ends (figure 14.1a).

- Spin up the end (figure 14.1b), double and ply back at the colour change (figure 14.1c) and tape the ends. Cut free from the anchor, and repeat with each pair.

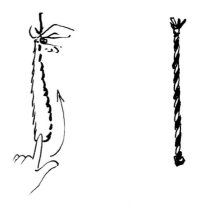

Figure 14.1c, d

- Firmly knot the folded end of each cord so when the beads are threaded they won't fall off (figure 14.1d).

To paint the beads:

beads of different shapes (you can use any shaped
    beads; craft and bead shops stock numerous
    shapes (see shopping guide)

undercoat sealer

gesso

acrylic paints (see materials list)

high gloss varnish

paint brushes (1 fine tip, 1 thick)

water

satay and chop sticks

- Place beads on chopsticks or satay sticks for
  easy handling.
- In turn paint all the beads using the thick
  brush with undercoat, then gesso to provide a
  good base. Wash each with a watery coat of
  paint, randomly mixing the colours.
- Paint some beads with a little stronger paint to
  decorate with spots and stripes using the fine
  brush.
- When dry, coat each with 2 or more coats of
  high gloss varnish.
- Thread each cord with the same type and
  number of beads to make 12 drops (figure
  14.2).

THE ROPE

To make the rope:

1 m (1 ⅛ yards) warp x 6 ends rayon thread (two
    shades of gold) (4 lengths)

1 m (1 ⅛ yards) warp x 6 ends Perle 5 (pink)
    (2 lengths)

1 m (1 ⅛ yards) warp x 6 ends Perle 5 (green)
    (2 lengths)

- The rope is a 4-segment double-twisted. The
  end is not attached to a wire as the hole at the
  top of the form is big enough for the rope to fit
  through.
- Refer to Example A on page 18 for instructions
  to make the rope.

To attach the rope to the form:

Figure 14.2

button or bead with large hole

strong sewing thread

wool needle

scissors

- Both ends of the rope are threaded through the
  hole at the top of the form, and pulled so as to
  make the taped ends even. Pull enough
  through to make a comfortable working length
  (figure 14.3).
- Thread the ends onto the bead or button and
  knot the ends together tightly (figure 14.4).
  Pull the knot hard against the bead.
- Thread the one free wire from the end of the
  underskirt onto the needle. Sew the wire
  through the rope to attach the skirt just above
  the bead (figure 14.5).
- Hold the wires up and wind the skirt in a very
  close spiral onto the rope, twist the loop end of
  the wire with the free ends (one that has the
  needle) tightly together to secure (figure 14.6).
  Cut the wires and turn the sharp ends in
  (detail of figure 14.6).
- Wrap binding of cotton thread 1 cm wide
  neatly and firmly over the top of the skirt to
  provide a neat firm base to attach the beaded
  drops (figure 14.7). Pull the rope up sharply to

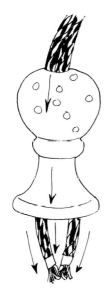

Figure 14.3

Figure 14.4

lock the skirt in place housed in the top of the ceramic head, steam and comb the skirt. Then trim the bottom edge so it is level (figure 14.8).

- Pull the skirt down again to expose the join area.

To attach the beads.
bead drops
Nymo (D)

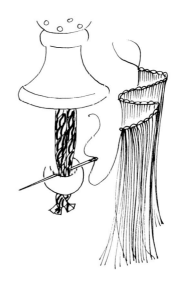

Figure 14.5

Figure 14.6

milliners needle
felt-tipped pen
high impact glue

- To make sure you have the bead drop lengths even hold one drop up and measure the length from where it is to be attached at the top to be level with the lower edge of the skirt.
- Mark the point at the top on the cord with a

Figure 14.7

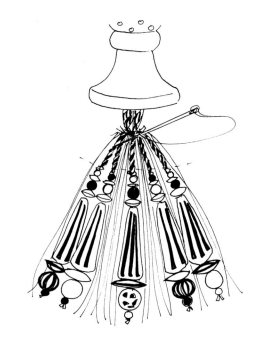

Figure 14.9

Figure 14.8

felt-tipped pen. Use this as a template and mark the others.

- Sew each of the cords neatly and securely at the pen mark to the band of thread (figure 14.9).
- Run a line of glue sparingly around where the cords are joined to the rope. When dry, trim the cord ends just above the line of glue. Once again pull the rope up tightly to house the skirt in the head of the form.
- Make an overhand knot in the rope, work it down to sit tightly, locking the skirt hard in the hollow form (figure 14.10).

Figure 14.10

CHAPTER 15

Beatrice

This tassel has a plain head with a gilded lozenge-shaped bead at the top. On this sits another silk-covered bead.

The ruff at the waist is made from covered metal flowers with silk-covered beads in the centre.

The underskirt is the basic tassel skirt, with a ribbon skirt fitted over this.

The petal embellishment on top of the ribbon skirt is made in a similar fashion to the metal flowers. They are covered with fine silk fabric, then silk thread embellishment is worked over the top. They are edged with beads. Beads covered with silk thread hold the petals in place on the skirt.

The rope is a simple three-part twisted to an S ply.

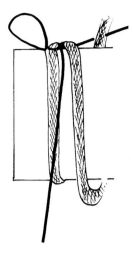

Figure 15.4

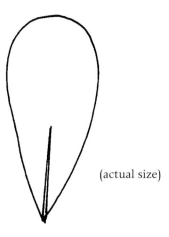

(actual size)

Figure 15.5

- Keep the ribbon neat and parallel. Repeat winding the ribbon around the board. Wire tightly to give a space between each loop until all the ribbon is used (figure 15.4).

To attach the ribbon skirt:
The ribbon skirt is attached after the basic under-skirt, and fits around the waist only once. After twisting tightly trim the wires close to the twist.

To make skirt petals (7):
25 cm (10 in) jap silk (for backing)
10 cm (4 in) fine silk fabric (blue)
16 cm (6¼ in) embroiderers hoop
heavy tracing paper
spray adhesive
aluminium sheet (can opened flat)
sharp pencil
beading needle
Nymo (D)
Gumnut yarns in colours given
175 (approx.) pink glass beads
175 (approx.) gold beads

To make the petals (7):
- Place backing silk into hoop, making it taut and wrinkle-free. Tighten screw.
- Trace petal pattern onto tracing paper from template (figure 15.5). Lightly spray the back

of the paper with adhesive spray and position on aluminium. Cut out petals and make 2.5 cm (1 in) cut into each petal. Overlap the edges and bind tightly with Nymo to make a slightly convex shape (figure 15.6).

Figure 15.6

- Trace the petal pattern onto the wrong side of the blue silk, then pencil a second outline 0.75 cm (⅓ in) larger than the original (make 7). Cut each out on the larger pencil line.
- Thread milliners needle with 30 cm (12 in) of Nymo, double and knot the end. Sew a small running stitch 4 mm (⅕ in) from the edge (figure 15.7). Pull up the running stitch to make a snug silk cover on the petal shape. Backstitch to secure (figure 15.8).

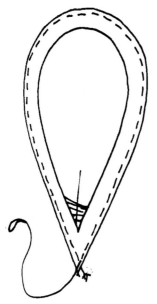

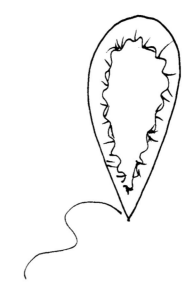

Figure 15.7

Figure 15.8

- Lightly spray the wrong side of the aluminium shape and place the sticky side down on the silk backing.
- Tack the petals onto the backing material in

the hoop. Satin stitch the pattern, working 3 stitches on an angle one way, then 3 on the opposite angle. Change colours and repeat (figure 15.9).

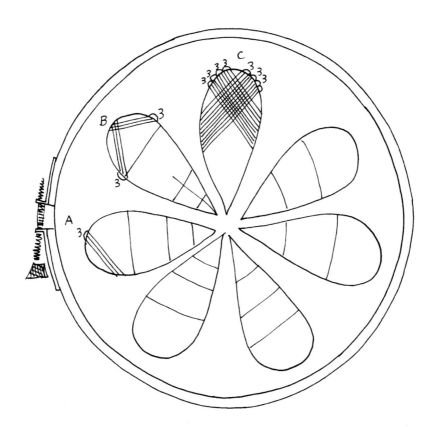

Figure 15.9

TASSELS

- Change colours on the wrong side of the work. Work a small double stitch to end and a neat knot to begin a new colour.
- Cut the shapes from the hoop. Thread approximately 25 of each bead type onto Nymo (figure 15.10a). Couch to the edge of each petal using Nymo and a fine milliners needle (figure 15.10b).

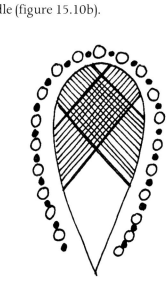

Figure 15.10a

Figure 15.10b

To cover the skirt beads (7):
7 pony (jug) beads
Gumnut yarns in colours given
milliners needle (no. 9)

- Thread silk onto needle, double thread, knot ends neatly. Pass thread through the hole and lock in place by taking needle through the loop at the knot. Wrap the thread tightly over the outside through the hole until the bead is covered.

- Pass the needle through the thread in the centre to fix the last wrap. Pull tightly and cut thread flush with the bead.

To assemble the skirt petals and beads:
- Wind a firm band of thread at the waist of the form to provide a neat surface to attach the petals and ruff.
- Sew the petals to the waist. Space them evenly. The metal shape can be bent to sit neatly.
- Sew a covered pony bead between each of the petals to hold them in place (figure 15.11).

Figure 15.11

THE FLOWER RUFF

To make the jasmine flowers (9):
25 cm (10 in) jap silk (backing)
16 cm (6¼ in) embroiderers hoop
Gumnut yarns (colours as given)
heavy tracing paper
spray adhesive

aluminium can opened flat
Nymo (D)
fine needle
wool needle
pencil
fine sharp scissors
sharp-nosed pliers

- Set backing material into the embroidery hoop so it is free from wrinkles.
- Trace 9 flower patterns onto tracing paper from template drawing (figure 15.12).

- Lightly spray the back of the traced pattern with adhesive spray, and position on aluminium. Cut out the metal petals and flowers. Lightly spray the backs of the cutouts and position one at a time on the silk material on the hoop (figure 15.13).
- Tack in position with a few holding stitches over the metal (figure 15.14).

(actual size)

Figure 15.12

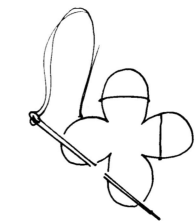

Figure 15.14

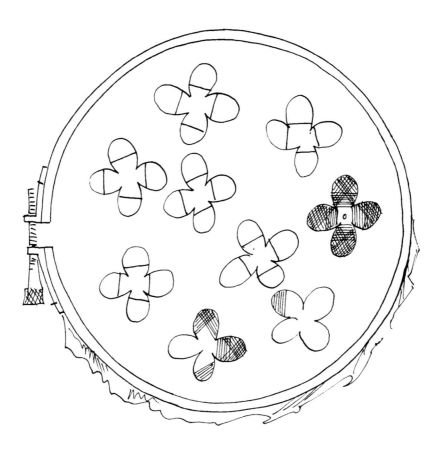

Figure 15.13

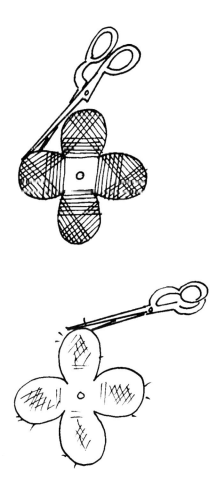

Figure 15.15a, b, c

Figure 15.16a, b

- Satin stitch to cover the entire shape using Gumnut yarns (figure 15.15a, b, c).
- Use wool needle to make a hole in the centre of each flower. Cut shape from the hoop with scissors (figure 15.16a), taking care not to cut stitching. Trim any excess silk fabric thread from the edges of flowers (figure 15.16b).

To cover the 10 mm (²⁄₅ in) beads (9):
9 x 10 mm (²⁄₅ in) beads
Gumnut yarns (colours as given)
milliners needle

- Place beads on satay sticks.
- Cover the beads with Gumnut yarns using the method as in Nina (page 22). Spray once only.

To assemble the flowers:
9 flower shapes

9 x 10 mm (²⁄₅ in) covered beads
Nymo
milliners needle
9 gold beads

- Thread 30 cm (12 in) of Nymo onto needle, double it and make a large knot. Pass needle through centre hole to the front of the flower, and thread covered bead, then gold bead (figure 15.17a). Then sew back through the covered bead and the centre of the flower, pull both ends of the thread tight and sew through silk cover at the base. Tie the two ends to secure and remove the needle (figure 15.17b). Leave two lengths of thread to attach the flowers to the waist later (figure 15.17c).
- Bend the petals into a cup shape using sharp nosed pliers (figure 15.17d).

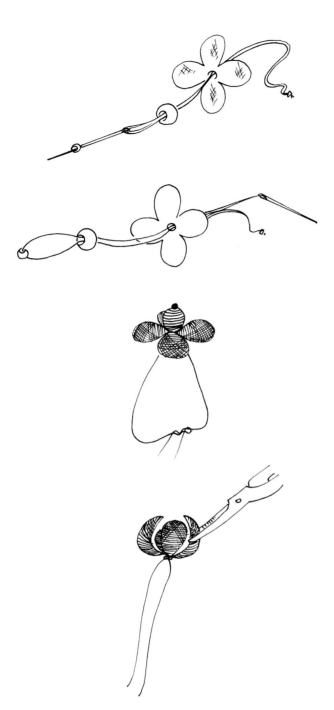

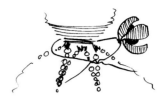

Figure 15.18

THE ROPE

1 m (1 ⅛ yards) warp x 16 ends rayon thread (both shades of gold)

1 m (1 ⅛ yards) warp x 16 ends Perle 5 (pink)

1 m (1 ⅛ yards) warp x 16 ends Perle 5 (green)

winding device

masking tape

scissors

- The rope is made 3-parts twisted, then plied to a simple rope.
- Make a 16 end warp by using 2 ends rayon thread 8 times over a warping measure of 1 m (1 ⅛ yards).
- The Perle colours should be warped 16 times each (separately) over a warping measure of 1 m (1 ⅛ yards).
- See cord and rope making for Nina tassel (page 26).

To attach the wire to the rope:
- Refer to Nina (page 26) for the materials and method of the wire attachment.

Figure 15.17a, b, c, d

To attach the flower ruff:
- Tie each flower around the waist tightly, using the threads attached to the flowers (figure 15.18). The first tie should be a non-slip knot followed by a further three knots on top. Trim excess thread close to the knot.
- Evenly space the flowers.

CHAPTER 16

Primavera

The form of this large tassel has a light wash of base colour
to which decoupage and gilding have been added.

The simple skirt is made from dyed mop cotton.

The three-part rope is simple and is also made
from dyed mop cotton.

The ruff is a fine twisted cord wound round
the waist of the tassel.

134 m (147²⁄₅ yards) mop cotton

wooden form no. 12
Jo Sonja acrylic paint—titanium white, gold,
    blue
gesso
water-based sealer—for example high gloss
    Crystal Clear
patterned paper—small pattern is recommended
1 x Dylon dye (blue)
1 x Dylon dye (green)
1 x Dylon dye (pink)
2.25 m (2½ yards) hobby wire
20 cm (8 in) 1.6 gauge aluminium wire

Figure 16.1

THE FORM

To paint the form:
form
acrylic paint
paintbrush (medium)
undercoat gesso
water-based sealer
water
sharp fine scissors
patterned paper
sandpaper—fine
PVA glue
soft cloth

- Sand the form and paint it with undercoat and
  then base colour.
- Gently sandpaper the back of the patterned
  paper until it is almost transparent to reduce
  the number of sealing layers needed to hide
  the cut edges. Cut out the patterns.
- Paint the back of the paper with PVA glue and
  place onto the form. Rub gently with fingers or
  soft cloth in a circular fashion to bond and
  remove any air bubbles (figure 16.1).
- Create a latticed pattern with gold paint to link
  your design. Paint gold band at the top where
  the rope enters the head (figure 16.2).

Figure 16.2

- Seal with several layers of the water-based
  sealer, drying well and sanding lightly
  between each coat. Use a soft cloth to remove
  any dust.

THE SKIRT

12 m (13⅕ yards) warp x 6 ends of mop cotton
Dylon dye (blue)
2.25 m (2½ yards) hobby wire

18 cm (7 $\frac{1}{5}$ in) skirt template
masking tape
sharp scissors
(Enough skirt should be made so as to allow for the skirt to go around the waist 2 or 3 times.)

To make the skirt:
- Wind the mop cotton into a neat hank to dye and tie off loosely three times to stop the hank becoming tangled.
- Dye the skirt threads in a very weak solution of Dylon dye, following the manufacturer's instructions.
- Follow the instructions for making the Nina skirt (page 23).
- Follow the method for attaching the Nina skirt to the form (page 28).
- Bind waist firmly with thread to provide a neat base for the ruff.

THE ROPE

3 x 2 m (2 $\frac{1}{5}$ yards) warp x 6 ends of mop cotton
20 cm (8 in) 1.6 gauge aluminium wire
Dylon dyes (green, pink and blue)
anchor
scissors
pliers
needle
sewing cotton

- In turn, dye up each section of mop cotton using a very weak solution of Dylon dye and following the manufacturer's instructions.
- Make the rope according to the 3-part rope instructions (page 16). Attach wire to the rope and the rope to the form as in the instructions for Nina (page 26).

THE RUFF

2 m (2 $\frac{1}{5}$ yards) mop cotton
Dylon dye (green)
winding device
anchor

- Dye thread following the manufacturer's instructions.
- Fold thread in half and attach to stable anchor. Spin up the ends in turn and ply back to even balance.

To attach the ruff to the waist:
- Neatly sew one free end of the cord to the waist of the tassel with Nymo and wind the cord tightly and neatly around it, tuck the free end in and fix in place with a neat stitch (figure 16.3).

Figure 16.3

CHAPTER 17

Lucrezia Borgia

This tassel uses many methods so far employed in the book.
If you feel confident that you have mastered these,
you will enjoy the challenge.

The head of the tassel is made up of four different parts, each
using a different method to cover the form. The base form is
covered with red gimp and edged at the top and bottom with
spun metal strips. The spindle is covered with fine red cord and
trimmed with green spun metal strip. The base of the next
segment, like the spindle, has a fine blue twisted cord. The
border between the blue cord and the green has a band of
blue silk thread onto which jasmine flowers are sewn.
The cylinder at the top is covered with blue silk thread
and gold gimp. There is an uncovered form

under the skirt to serve as a platform for the skirts to sit on.

There are 5 parts to the skirt: a rayon underskirt (gold), a double-twisted bullion overskirt (gold gimp), a twice-twisted two-coloured layer (gold and red gimp), blue single-twisted cords, and a jasmine petal peplum.

The rope is four-part and double-twisted, with a dividing cylinder covered with needle weaving.

All the covered forms and skirt parts are threaded onto the wire of the rope, before being secured at the base.

REQUIREMENTS

1 reel YLI Pearl Crown Rayon no. 771 (gold)
2 reels YLI Pearl Crown Rayon no. 772 (gold)
2 hanks DMC Perle 3 no. 798 (blue)
1 hank DMC Perle 5 no. 333 (purple)
2 hanks DMC Perle 5 no. 666 (red)
1 hank DMC Perle 5 no. 3046 (gold)
1 hank DMC Perle 5 no. 909 (green)
1 hank DMC Perle 5 no. 798 (blue)
35 m (38 ½ yards) Mokuba Gimp no. 15 (gold)
15 m (16 ½ yards) Mokuba Gimp no. 66 (red)
5 spirals Madeira silk no. 0210 (red)
3 spirals Madeira silk no. 1102 (blue)
2 spirals Madeira silk no. 0206 (orange)
2 spirals Madeira silk no. 1214 (green)
1 spiral Madeira silk no. 0902 (purple)
85 cm (34 in) perl perl (see glossary)
50 cm (20 in) jap silk (backing fabric)

wooden form no. 8
wooden spindle form no. 6
wooden form no. 7
wooden form no. 9 (uncovered)
15 cm (6 in) embroiderers hoop
4 m (4 ⅖ yards) hobby wire
20 cm (8 in) 2 mm ($\frac{1}{16}$ in) wire

THE FORM

To cover the base form:
form no. 8

2.5 m (2 ¾ yards) red gimp
spray adhesive

- The base form is covered with red gimp using the same technique as for Nina (page 22).

To make covered metal strips:
covering thread (blue, green silk)
high impact glue
20 cm (8 in) x 4 mm ($\frac{1}{5}$ in) aluminium strip
sharp scissors
paper cutting scissors
milliners needle
ruler
felt-tipped pen

- Open and flatten an empty aluminium can. Using a felt-tipped pen, rule off into 3 mm ($\frac{1}{8}$ in) strips and cut neatly with paper scissors.
- Using the blue silk thread, attach an end to one end of a 20 cm (8 in) aluminium strip with glue. Wind the thread evenly to cover 5 cm (2 in) of the strip, and glue the end of the blue silk safely. Then join the green silk to cover the rest of the strip. Glue the end to secure and cut the thread flush with the strip.
- Cut the blue end from the strip.
- Put the prepared strips aside until the form is assembled.

To cover the spindle:
spindle form no. 6
4 m (4 ⅖ yards) Madeira silk (red)
anchor
2 m (2 ⅕ yards) Madeira silk (green)
14 cm (5 ⅔ in) x 4 mm ($\frac{1}{5}$ in) aluminium strip
spray adhesive

- Fold red Madeira thread in half and loop over a stable anchorage. Twist both free ends until ready to kink. Join and twist back to even balance, making the cord to cover the spindle.
- Finely coat the spindle once with spray adhesive.
- Cover the spindle with the prepared red cord.

- Cover the metal strip with green silk, following the instructions as for green and blue strip but do not cut.

To cover the larger form:
form no. 7
Madeira silk threads, blue, green, orange, red
other materials as to cover Nina tassel (page 22)

- Use the same method to cover the form as for Nina (page 22).
- Twist 3 m (3⅓ yards) blue silk to make cord to cover the lower part of the form. Make the stripe pattern with the remaining colours, un-twisted, changing colours where the shape changes. Cut thread with scissors and butt each new colour against the end of the old.

To cover the cylinder form:
2 cm (⅘ in) cut from the end of a spent fax roll
2 m (2⅕ yards) Madeira silk, blue
50 cm (20 in) gold gimp
wool needle

- Thread the needle with the silk, double and knot the end. The inside hole of the fax cylinder is large enough to make it easy to thread the needle through to cover the outside.
- Start by threading the needle through the centre of the hole and passing it back through the knotted end to secure (make sure the knot is in the centre not on the outside).
- Wrap the thread through the centre and over the outside until it is covered neatly.
- Run the needle through the centre threads to finish and cut flush with the end of the hole.
- Thread the needle with the gimp and sew through a few threads in the centre to catch. Stripe the blue silk covering with gold gimp.

To make jasmine flowers (5):
Madeira silk (blue)
5 strips 3 mm (⅛ in) x 10.8 cm (4⅓ in) cut from can
2.5 cm (1 in) template

Nymo
milliners needle
high impact glue
sharp scissors
sharp-nosed pliers

- Spray the aluminium lightly with spray adhesive, and let it become 'high tack'. Bond the end of blue silk thread onto one end of the metal strip and wind the thread carefully and neatly from one end to the other, so no metal is visible underneath (figure 17.1a, b).

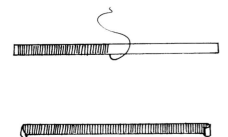

Figure 17.1a, b

- Use 2.5 cm (1 in) template to make 4 or 5-petal flowers starting and finishing 2 mm (¹⁄₁₆ in) beyond the centre (figure 17.2). Trim excess length. Remove from template.

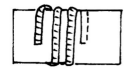

Figure 17.2

- Bind the centre tightly with Nymo and sew through the centre of the binding to secure (figure 17.3). Do not remove thread as it is used to sew centres in place.
- Bend to shape with sharp-nosed pliers (figure 17.4).

Figure 17.3

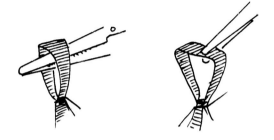

Figure 17.4

To make the centres (5):
25 cm (10 in) jap silk (backing fabric)
15 cm (6 in) embroiderers hoop
spray adhesive
Madeira silk (contrasting colours)
15 cm (6 in) perl perl
1 cm (²⁄₅ in) circle template

- Fit silk fabric into embroiderers hoop. Make taut.
- Trace 5 x 1 cm (²⁄₅ in) circles onto aluminium, cut out and lightly spray with glue.
- Place on fabric, thread needle with contrasting silk thread and satin stitch in a criss-cross pattern to densely cover the circle.
- Position a border of perl perl around the outside edge and couch in place, using one strand of silk (figure 17.5). Sew through cover to finish and cut thread flush with work.
- Cut circle close to perl perl using small sharp scissors.
- Sew the centres to the middle of the flowers (figure 17.6).
- Sew finished flowers to the band of blue silk thread on form no. 7.

Figure 17.5

Figure 17.6

THE SKIRTS

To make the underskirt:
10 m (11 yards) warp x 30 ends rayon (both shades of gold—2 x 771 to 1 x 772)
18 cm (7¹⁄₅ in) template
2 m (2¹⁄₅ yards) hobby wire
masking tape
scissors

- The underskirt is made as the tassel skirt of Nina (page 23). Follow the instructions and cut the skirt from the board.

To make the bullion-twisted overskirt:
20 m (22 yards) gold gimp
anchor
18 cm (7¹⁄₅ in) template
1.5 m (1²⁄₃ yards) hobby wire
battery-operated drill
masking tape
cylinder or board on which to wind the spun gimp

- Keep everything you need within reach—your cardboard cylinder, scissors, tape and drill. Also cut tape ready for use.
- Secure the gimp on a stable anchor. Place scissors and cut pieces of masking tape close by. Anchor the other end of the gimp securely in the chuck of the drill. Hold taut and spin

up the thread until it is wobbly and fighting hard against further twisting.

- Holding the tension, remove the twisted end from the drill and tape the ends securely to the cardboard cylinder. Maintaining tension, wind the twisted thread neatly onto the cylinder. Secure the other end with tape after removing it from the anchor, without losing the twist at the end.
- Leave the twists to 'set' for at least a day for easier management.

To wire the overskirt:
- Wire the overskirt using the method for Nina. Be neat and even as you wind the thread around the board. Start the skirt by attaching the wire to the end of the gimp without losing any of the twist.
- Finish securely with several twists of the wire.
- Slide each loop separately from the board and twist back to make the bullions. Bend the template and slide the work over close to its edge to make it easier to remove the loops.
- Steam the skirt over a boiling saucepan of steam to set twists. Use kitchen tongs or oven mitts to prevent scalding your hands.

To make the double-twisted bullion:
8 m (8⅘ yards) red gimp cut to 18 x 44 cm
    (17⅔ in) lengths
8 m (8⅘ yards) gold gimp cut to 18 x 44 cm
    (17⅔ in) lengths
high impact glue
stable anchor
sharp scissors

- It is best to start a little factory production line here. Count the number of twists you make in each cord if you are a perfectionist.
- Anchor the first gimp end securely and twist up until tight. Fold in half, maintaining the tension, and let it twist back. Tape the ends together. Repeat with one colour to have 18 cords.

- Securely anchor the taped ends. Thread the contrast colour through the loop end of the twisted section.
- If you have a cabler it is easy to twist up the two free ends. If not have a second person twist up one free end while you twist the other.
- Join the two when ready to kink, tape the ends and let this twist back to an even balance.
- Twist the whole length till tight then fold at the change in colour, and let the two colours twist back.
- Tape the two close to the end.
- Thread a milliners needle with Nymo and bind the end very firmly close to the tape. Leave a thread as you will need this to attach the cord.
- Place a dab of glue over the binding.
- Repeat with each length.
- When the glue is completely dry cut the cord just above the glue to make a neat end, being careful not to cut the thread.

To attach the double-twisted cords:
50 cm (20 in) hobby wire
Nymo
milliners needle

- The cords need to be fixed onto a circle of wire, so this can be threaded onto the rope wire. The cords are evenly spaced around the wire base.
- Wind the wire around the tips of your index and middle finger 4 times and twist the ends around to make a neat circle (figure 17.7).
- Sew each of the cords tightly and securely to the band of wire (figure 17.8).

To make the blue single-twisted cords:
2 hanks Perle 3, no. 798 (blue)
scissors
Nymo
milliners needle
glue
50 cm (20 in) hobby wire

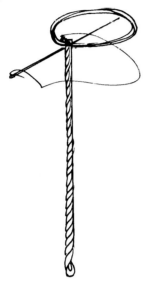

Figure 17.7

Figure 17.8

- Cut the hanks of Perle 3 and separate into groups of 4 ends.
- Twist up 4 ends, fold in half, and neatly secure the end with glue.
- Repeat until 12 cords have been made.
- Make a second wire circle using the hobby wire and attach the blue twisted cords neatly and safely, using a milliners needle.

To make the jasmine petal overskirt:
25 cm (10 in) jap silk (backing fabric)
15 cm (6 in) embroiderers hoop
Madeira silk (red)
perl perl
heavy tracing paper
aluminium sheet
Nymo
milliners needle (no. 9)
pencil
spray adhesive

- Place backing silk onto hoop and make taut.
- Trace peplum shape (figure 17.9) onto tracing paper. Spray lightly with adhesive and position on aluminium sheet.

(actual size)

Figure 17.9

TASSELS

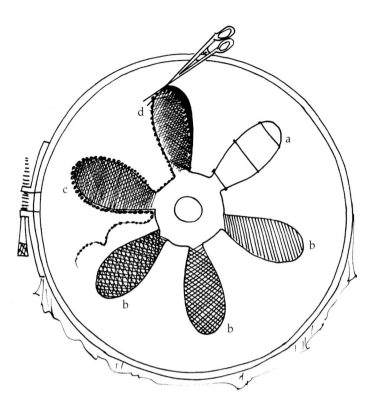

Figure 17.10a, b, c, d

- Cut out shape. Spray lightly with adhesive. Place on backing silk in hoop. Tack lightly in position (figure 17.10a).
- Cover each petal shape in turn with red silk using a close diagonal satin stitch (see glossary). Stitch first on one angle, then on the opposite, and finally parallel stitches until there is a dense cover (figure 17.10b).
- Couch perl perl around the outer edge with Nymo to form snug outline (figure 17.10c).
- Use sharp scissors to cut entire shape from the hoop (figure 17.10d).
- Bend gently into a cup shape.

THE ROPE

1.5 m (1⅔ yards) warp x 6 ends Perle 5 (red) (4 segments) (twisted up and plied back to make 2 red cords)
1.5 m (1⅔ yards) warp x 6 ends Perle 5 (purple)
1.5 m (1⅔ yards) warp x 6 ends Perle 5 (gold) (twisted up and plied back to make one purple and gold cord)

1.5 m (1⅔ yards) warp x 6 ends Perle 5 (green)
1.5 m (1⅔ yards) warp x 6 ends Perle 5 (blue) (twisted up and plied back to make a blue and green cord)

- Double twist these 4 segments. Anchor the 4 cords in this order: red, mixed, red, mixed. Twist on separately, ply back together to make the rope. Tape the ends and remove from the anchor.

THE ROPE CYLINDER

3 mm (⅛ in) x 6 cm (2⅖ in) aluminium strip
6 mm (¼ in) x 6 cm (2⅖ in) aluminium strip (two)
5 cm (2 in) cut from a spent fax cylinder centre
silk colours left over from covering the forms
milliners needle
wool needle
20 cm (8 in) x 2 mm (1/16 in) gauge wire to anchor the rope
masking tape
scissors
pliers

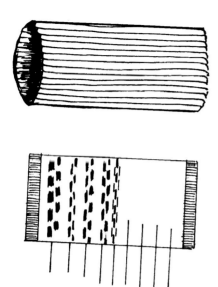

Figure 17.11a, b

- Cover the aluminium strips—the long one with red and the two short ones with green.
- Cover the cylinder along its length, first with orange silk using a wool needle, wrapping through the centre and over the top (figure 17.11a).
- Weave the contrasting colours around the cylinder, the first row going under two and over two (darning or weaving).
- To weave the second row, take a contrast colour. Stitch over where the previous row was under (figure 17.11b). Continue until the cylinder is woven completely. (Your stitching may be more perfect than mine. I needed to disguise my untidiness at the end by gluing covered metal strips at each end where I joined the new colours.)

To assemble the parts:
uncovered form no. 9
20 cm (8 in) x 2 mm ($\frac{1}{16}$ in) wire
pliers
Nymo

- Refer to figure 17.12.

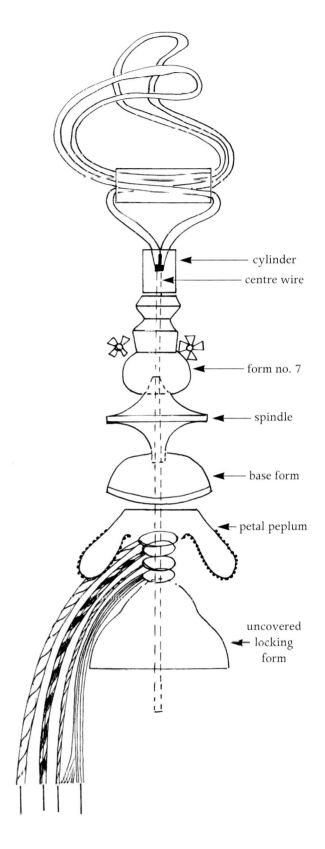

cylinder
centre wire
form no. 7
spindle
base form
petal peplum
uncovered locking form

Figure 17.12

- Thread the rope through the cylinder and slide the loops to be equal. Attach 2 mm ($\frac{1}{16}$ in) gauge wire to the rope following the rope attachment for Nina (page 26).
- Fit the skirts one at a time on top of the 'locking form': first the basic skirt, then the bullion twist, followed by the two-coloured gimp, the blue and the petal peplum.
- Thread the wire through the 4 covered form segments. Push the forms hard onto the skirts. Turn the end of the wire into a tight curl, using pliers to lock at the base of the form beneath the skirts.
- You will need to arrange the skirts neatly, and move the cords so they sit symmetrically (there should be two blues falling from between each petal of the peplum).
- Finally tighten the wire to lock the whole as one.
- You may need to place a binding of thread where the skirt joins the outside forms and neaten with the 15 cm (6 in) green strip around the base. Glue in place carefully with high impact glue.
- Bend the wire if necessary to align the segments of the form.

Chapter 18

Soraya

Experienced bead weavers will have no problems with this tassel. But be warned, bead weaving is time consuming and requires enormous patience.

The head of the form has been covered with off-loom bead weaving. The use of different coloured beads creates the patterns. Because I am an inexperienced bead weaver it was quite by accident that the flower pattern I created fitted the form perfectly. I was unable to increase without upsetting the pattern and so introduced larger beads.

Over the basic skirt there is an overskirt worked with several different shapes and sizes of coloured beads, a mix of old and new. The overskirt makes a lace-like pattern.

The rope is three-part and double twisted. It has a dividing cylinder covered with gimp and embellished with peyote stitch beading

The ruffs are made from a mixture of crystal, round, Delica and seed beads.

REQUIREMENTS

3 reels YLI Pearl Crown Rayon no. 811 (pink)

2.5 m (2 ¾ yards) Mokuba Gimp (pink)

1 pkt each of Mill Hill Antique Glass Beads,
    no. 03023 (dusty pink), no. 62041 (yellow)
    no. 00150 (pale blue)

5 g (⅕ ounce) each of Delica Beads, nos 416, 427
    (blue), no. 88 (pearl pink), no. 209 (mauve),
    no. 106 (pale pink), nos 380, 456, 22 (green),
    no. 12 (pink)

500 x 1 mm (1/32 in) square glass beads (silver-grey)

16 x 3 cm (1⅕ in) bugle beads (blue)

16 x 2 cm (⅘ in) bugle beads (blue)

26 x 6 mm (¼ in) round beads (pink)

60 x 6 mm (¼ in) crystal beads (blue)

60 x 6 mm (¼ in) crystal beads (green)

50 x 6 mm (¼ in) crystal beads (clear)

50 x 6 mm (¼ in) crystal beads (pale pink)

26 x 6 mm (¼ in) crystal beads (amber)

wooden form no. 1

1.5 m (1⅔ yards) hobby wire

15 cm (6 in) 1.6 aluminium wire

THE FORM

form

Nymo (D)

Mill Hill beads, dusty pink, yellow

Delica beads, colours as given

scissors

super glue

needle (size 12)

1 m (1⅛ yards) cotton thread

- Wind a band of cotton thread around the waist of the form and tie securely.
- Thread the needle with Nymo without knotting the end.
- Take the form and turn it upside down. Sew Nymo onto the band of the thread, close to the head. Tie a non-slip knot, place a dab of super

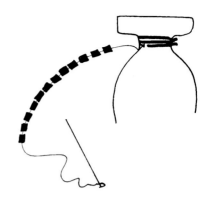

Figure 18.1

glue over the knot, let dry and pull tight to make sure that it is anchored safely.

- Thread onto Nymo a mix of blue Delica beads 416, 427 until you have enough to encircle the waist, less one bead (figure 18.1).
- Start the second row by picking up the first bead threaded, then every second (figure 18.2). Pull the thread tightly to start the 'brick' pattern (figure 18.3).

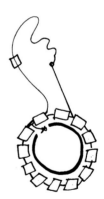

Figure 18.2

Figure 18.3

- As the form shape increases you may add 2 beads or, as I have done, introduce slightly larger Mill Hill seed beads to make a flower pattern.

To make the flower pattern:
- Work 7 seed beads in a flower shape over five rows (Mill Hill dusty pink for petals, yellow for centres).
  Row 1 One seed bead is picked up.
  Row 2 One is picked up each side of the first.
  Row 3 A single yellow bead in the middle of these two for the centre.
  Rows 4 and 5 Mirror image the first two rows to complete the flower.
- Continue using this method around the form.

To make the herringbone shape immediately following:
  Row 1 Alternate Delica beads, 88 (pearl pink) and 209 (mauve).
  Row 2 Start herringbone by working two beads of the same colour then continue to alternate the two colours, giving a check pattern on the next row.
- Continue until 6 rows are complete, then reverse the pattern to make a mirror image (5 rows).
- Work 5 plain rows using Delica 106 (pale pink), then 4 plain rows using Delica 456 (green).
- Work 3 rows of Delica 106 (pale pink). Repeat the flower pattern this time using Delica 456 (green) and 12 (pink).
- Work 3 rows Delica 106 (pale pink).
- Using Delica green (456) and pink (12) work 11 rows of the first part of the herringbone pattern to form a diagonal stripe.
- Work 10 rows 209 (mauve) and random flowers in dusty pink Mill Hill and Delica 427 (blue–centres).
- Continue working until the form is filled using greens (22, 380).

- Finish securely by running the needle through the last row of beads a second time then anchoring the end with super glue.

THE SKIRT

To make the underskirt:
8 m (8⅘ yards) warp x 27 ends rayon thread (pink) (pass 3 ends over 8 m/8⅘ yards measure 9 times)
11 cm (4⅖ in) template
1.5 m (1⅔ yards) hobby wire
other materials as for Nina (page 23)

- Follow the instructions to make the Nina underskirt (page 23).
- Attach the underskirt to the form according to the Nina method (page 28).

To make the beaded overskirt:
beads: silver-grey square glass, blue bugles (2 cm/⅘ in, 3 cm/1⅕ in), round pink, blue crystal, green crystal, pale pink crystal, amber crystal (quantities as given)
Nymo (D)
milliners needle (no. 9) or beading needle

- Follow the diagram (figure 18.4).
- Thread needle with Nymo and anchor securely to the waistband: first knot the end, then oversew at least four times. Pull tightly to lock the knot in place.
- The first 6 double bugle drops are made by following the diagram.
- In between space the 6 single bugle drops (see diagram).
- The linking strands are attached next (see diagram).

THE ROPE

1 m (1⅒ yards) warp x 5 ends rayon thread (6 lengths)
anchor
scissors

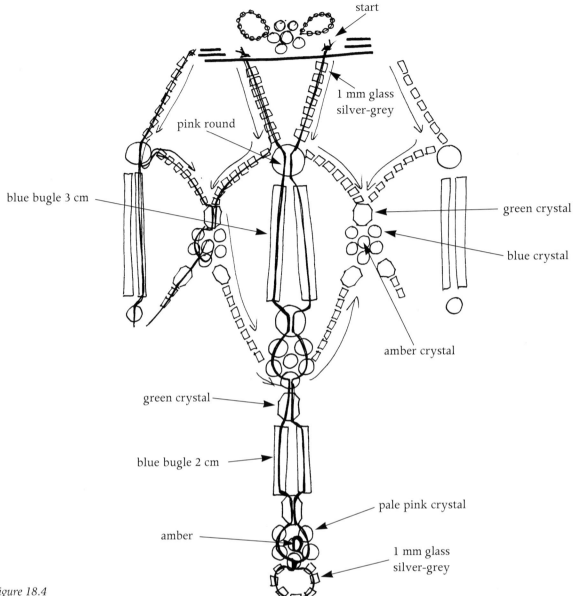

start

1 mm glass silver-grey

pink round

blue bugle 3 cm

green crystal

blue crystal

amber crystal

green crystal

blue bugle 2 cm

pale pink crystal

amber

1 mm glass silver-grey

Figure 18.4

masking tape
winding device

- Pair the lengths. Anchor one pair and twist up separately until ready to kink. Join and ply back. Repeat with the remaining two pairs.
- The three segments are twisted separately again on the same rotation, joined and plied back to complete the double-twisted rope.
- Tape each end and remove from anchor.

To make the dividing cylinder:
4 cm (1⅔ in) length cut from spent fax cylinder

2.5 m (2¾ yards) pink gimp
Delica beads, green (456)
Mill Hill beads, pale blue
beading materials as above
other materials used to cover basic Nina form
    (page 22)

- Cover the cylinder with gimp as for Nina form (page 22).
- Work 6 rows of peyote stitch ('brick' pattern, page 120) each end of the cylinder.

To attach the rope:

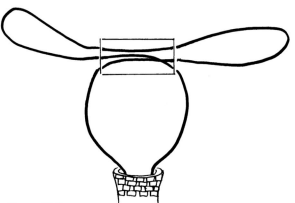

Figure 18.5

15 cm (6 in) 1.6 aluminium wire
pliers
needle
strong sewing thread

- Thread the rope through to make a loop on each side of the cylinder. Slide the loops so they are equal (figure 18.5). Attach the rope to the wire and join it to the form using the same method as Snow Queen (page 42).

THE RUFFS

remaining Delica beads
seed beads
crystals
round beads
Nymo
no. 12 needle

To make the waist ruff:
- Make flowers by anchoring thread at the binding on the base of the form. Thread 5 of the same colour beads on the needle. Pass the needle through 2 or 3 of the beads twice.
- Push the bead circle so it sits close onto the waist. Thread a centre bead onto the needle and secure firmly by sewing into the band of thread at the waist (figure 18.6).
- String 5 or 6 of 1 mm ($^1/_{32}$ in), or 10 or 11 Mill Hill seed beads together onto the needle and sew back to make a loop (figure 18.7). Repeat,

Figure 18.6

Figure 18.7

using a variety of colours and beads, until the space is full.

To make the rope ruff:
- The rope ruff has been worked in a similar manner. A base of thread will need to be wrapped at the junction of the head and rope to provide a base onto which the bead flowers can be sewn.
- Single large beads are fixed in place by passing the needle through the hole, then through a small bead. Pass the needle back through the large bead and anchor firmly (figure 18.8a, b).

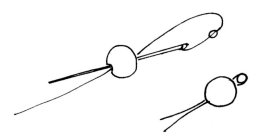

Figure 18.8a, b

CHAPTER 19

Tara

This turk's head knot is seen as an addition to decorate the rope or cover a join. It could be used as a skirt embellishment. It may also be used as the top for small tassels, particularly as an accent on clothing and scarves. It would work well in a group as a key tassel.

REQUIREMENTS

1.5 m (1⅔ yards) Mokuba Gimp
20 cm (8 in) YLI Pearl Crown Rayon
65 cm (26 in) silk velvet chenille

THE HEAD

1.5 m (1⅔ yards) gimp
4 cm (1⅔ yards) x 6 mm (¼ in) dowel or pencil

To make the head:

- The head is formed by the turk's head knot.
- Make a loop at one end of the cord (figure 19.1) and turn from 12 o'clock to 9 o'clock.

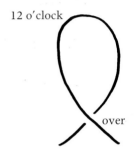

Figure 19.1

- Take the long end and make a second loop of the same size (figure 19.2) to overlap the first. The short free end lies across the long end. Turn work again a little.

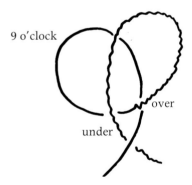

Figure 19.2

- Still working with the long free end make the third loop by weaving it over the first part of the second loop, then under then over and under (figure 19.3).

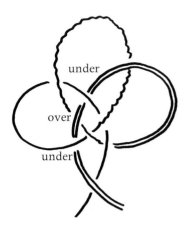

Figure 19.3

Figure 19.4

- You should now have 3 complete loops and one broken one that is formed by the 2 free ends (figure 19.4). Take the long free end again and trace the same pattern weaving its end in and out until three strands of cord match side by side (figure 19.5).

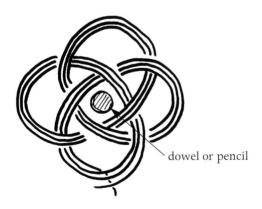

Figure 19.5

TASSELS

[*126*]

- Transfer work onto a pencil or dowel and pull the pattern into a cylindrical shape as you would to tighten loose shoelaces.

THE CORD

20 cm (8 in) rayon thread

- The thread is spun up, kink twisted and the ends knotted, to make a very fine cord.

THE SKIRT

65 cm (26 in) chenille
5 cm (2 in) template
Nymo (D)
milliners needle
To make the skirt:

- Set the cord at the top edge of the template. Wind the chenille around the template evenly (figure 19.6).

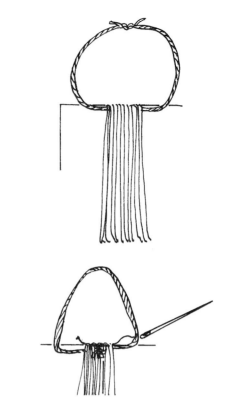

Figure 19.7a, b

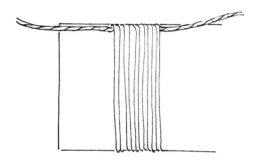

Figure 19.6

- Tie the ends of the cord together securely (figure 19.7a) and slide the knot to disappear into the skirt.
- Thread the needle with Nymo, double and knot the ends. Sew through the top of the skirt (figure 19.7b).
- Slide the skirt gently from the board, hold the cord out of the way and bind the top area of the skirt close to the cord to secure the top (figure 19.8).

dab of glue

Figure 19.8   *Figure 19.9*

To assemble the tassel:

Thread the cord through the turk's head. Apply a dob of glue at the area bound with the Nymo to secure it safely (figure 19.9), or simply knot the cord to lock the top of the skirt in its turk's head house.

CHAPTER 20

Gen-May

This is a Japanese knot often seen in pairs on bamboo blinds. It may be used as a key tassel.

The form is a little plastic blind pull. It is hollow and makes a good tassel form. It is covered with rayon thread and embellished with detached buttonhole stitch.

REQUIREMENTS

16 m (17⅔ yards) YLI Pearl Crown Rayon no. 241
(red)

4 m (4⅖ yards) Madeira Metallic Thread no. 40
(gold)

3 m (3⅓ yards) DMC Perle 5 (red) (optional)

1 cup-shaped plastic blind pull

75 cm (30 in) hobby wire

THE FORM

plastic blind pull

1 m (1⅛ yards) rayon thread (red)

other materials as for covering Nina form
(page 22)

metallic thread (gold)

milliners needle (no. 9)

- Cover the plastic form as for the Nina tassel
  (page 22). Spray once only.
- Starting at the opening at the bottom, work
  detached buttonhole stitch in gold over the
  surface of the form. Refer if necessary to
  Bohemia, page 48, for instructions for this
  stitch.

THE SKIRT

2 m (2⅕ yards) warp x 6 ends rayon thread (red)

7 cm (2⅘ in) template

75 cm (30 in) hobby wire

scissors

- Follow the method used for the skirt of Nina
  (page 23).

THE ROPE

4 m (4⅖ yards) rayon thread (red)

3 m (3⅓ yards) Perle 5 (red)

To make the cord:

Make either a firm double-twisted cord 75 cm (30
in) long or, as I have done here, spin a cover of
rayon thread tightly over 4 ends x 75 cm (30 in)
red Perle 5. As long as the cord is hard it will work.

To make the knot:

- Place the cord on a flat surface in front of you.
  Fold it two thirds along its length to make a
  loop at the fold a) (figure 20.1).

Figure 20.1

- Take the free short end over the top and down
  behind loop a) to make loop b) (figure 20.2).

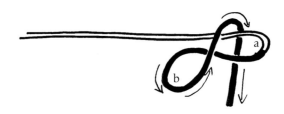

Figure 20.2

- Make a loop c) using the long free end and
  pass it through loop a) to make loop d) (figure
  20.3).

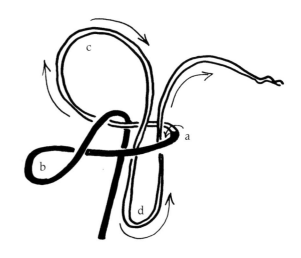

Figure 20.3

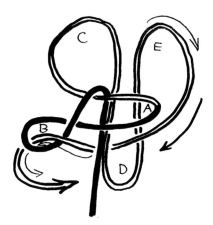

Figure 20.4

- Take the free end and pass through loop d), then in front of the other free short end, and pass through loop b) (figure 20.4).
- Bring long free end back behind the short free end through loop d) (figure 20.5).

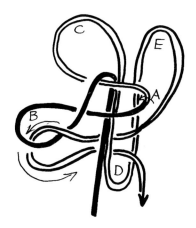

Figure 20.5

- Tighten the knot holding the free ends, and open the loops b), c) and e) to create equal loop sizes. You should have created a square in the middle of the three loops (figure 20.6).

To assemble the tassel:
- Tie a firm overhand knot about 1 cm (²⁄₅ in) below the square dragonfly knot.
- Thread the two ends through the hole at the top of the form.

Figure 20.6

- Wind the skirt tightly around the uncut ends of the cord, leaving the two free ends long enough to make a knot. Squeeze a dob of glue inside the head of the form, gently slide the skirt up to be housed inside the head.
- When glue is dry, tie the two free ends of the cord tightly against the inner top of the form and cut close to the knot.

Glossary

couching —outlining an image with a line of thick thread that lies on top of the fabric. The thick thread is held in place at even intervals with holding stitches of a finer thread (see diagram).

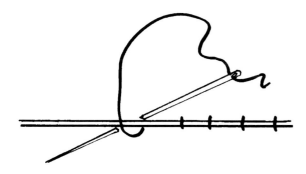

Couching

bullion—a thread twisted up tightly and then twisted back on itself, making a kink-twisted cord with an uncut end.

decoupage—cutting and pasting patterns onto a surface that is then covered with many layers of varnish to obliterate the cut edges.

dividing knot—an embracing knot used to hold back a curtain.

ends—the term for the thread count in a warp.

embroidery floss—a fine silk or cotton thread used for embroidery.

form or mould—the wooden part or parts of a tassel. A form may be ceramic.

french knot—a neat knot on top of a surface, with no thread only visible. Bring thread out at position of first knot. Take a small stitch beside the thread exit without removing needle. Wind thread around needle twice,

clockwise. Hold stitch firmly with left thumb. Pull needle free and pull out while still keeping knot under your thumb. Tighten the knot down onto the surface with your left thumbnail. Stab needle close to base of new knot and bring it out where you are ready to make the next french knot (see diagram).

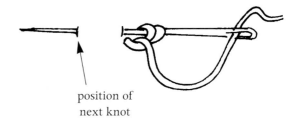

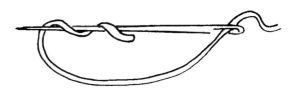

position of
next knot

gimp—a cotton core, overspun with a covering thread of silk, cotton or rayon.

lazy daisy—the stitch used as flower petals or leaves. The needle is taken through at a) for the beginning of the first stitch. Hold the thread down with your left thumb to start a loop.

French knot

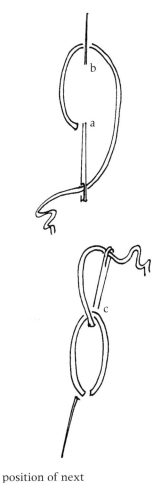

mainly in ecclesiastical gold work. Purchase
from regalia suppliers.

peyote stitch—an off-loom, needle weaving, bead
stitch. Full instructions for this stitch are to be
found in Soraya, page 120.

satin stitch—a straight stitch, smoothly and
evenly worked, each stitch close and parallel
to the one above. Used to fill a shape with solid
colour.

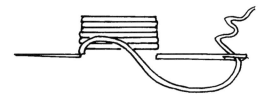

Satin stitch

template—a pattern, usually a thin plate of wood,
metal, plastic or cardboard.

warping—the process combining a group of
threads of even length and tension that can be
used together as one.

wrapping—the process winding thread or gimp
around an object, such as a large bead or a
wooden form.

position of next
petal or leaf

Lazy daisy

Reinsert the needle at a). Bring out at b). Pull
needle through and pull loop into position. Do
not pull too tightly. Make couching stitch into
c). Bring needle out where you wish to position the next leaf (see diagram).

perl perl—a very fine gold or silver spring, used

Suppliers

SUPPLIERS, KITS AND CLASSES

VICTORIA

Metropolitan

Susan Dickens Workshop
  6 Kensington Rd
  South Yarra 3141
  Tel/Fax (03) 9826 8155
  Web Site: sdtassels@telstra.easymail.com.au
Bustles & Bows
  164 Union St
  Surrey Hills 3127
  Tel. (03) 9888 5018
  and
  301 Wattletree Rd
  Malvern East 3145
  Tel. (03) 9576 1539
Kaye Pyke
  118 Bridge St
  Port Melbourne 3207
  Tel. (03) 9646 3540
Romantique
  68 Milton Pde
  Malvern 3144
  Tel. (03) 9822 5293

Country

Attic Crafts
  98 Queen St
  Bendigo 3550
  Tel. (03) 5441 7333
Sovereign Needlecraft
  215 Mair St
  Ballarat 3350
  Tel. (03) 5332 1782

NEW SOUTH WALES

Metropolitan

The Crewel Goblin
  5 Marian St
  Killara 2071
  Tel. (02) 9498 6831
Kirri Toose Design Studio
  117–119 Pacific Highway
  Cowan 2081
  Tel. (02) 9456 4275

Country

Sew & Tell
  Shop 2/118 Queen St
  Berry 2535
  Tel. (02) 4464 2428

QUEENSLAND

Miller & Coates
  Corner Beatrice Tce and Seymour St
  Ascot 4007
  Tel. (07) 3268 3955

AUSTRALIAN CAPITAL TERRITORY

Affinity Plus
  Cosmopolitan Court, 64 Wollongong St
  Fyshwick 2609
  Tel. (02) 6239 3322

SOUTH AUSTRALIA

Needleworld
  107 King William Rd
  Hyde Park 5061
  Tel. (08) 8272 0151

TASMANIA

The Needlewoman

63 Melville St
Hobart 7000
Tel. (03) 6234 3966

Petit Point
Shop 19 Yorketown Square,
Launceston 7250
Tel. (03) 6231 2021

THREADS

Cotton on Creations
(contact for retail outlet for Pearl Crown
Rayon)
PO Box 804
Epping, NSW 2121
Tel. (02) 9868 4253
Fax. (02) 9868 4269

Gumnut Yarns
164 Union St
Surrey Hills, Vic 3127
Tel. (03) 9888 5018
and
301 Wattletree Rd
Malvern East Vic 3145
Tel. (03) 9576 1539

Littlewood Fleece Yarns
RMB 2250
Euroa, Vic 3666
Tel. (03) 5795 1661

Penguin Thread
(Madeira Products)
25–27 Izett St
Prahran, Vic 3181
Tel. (03) 9529 4400

Romantique
(Benz Crown Rayon Thread)
68 Milton Pde
Malvern, Vic 3144

Taxtor Trading
(wool cotton, chenille, rayon etc.)
15 Brighton St
Richmond, Vic 3121
Tel. (03) 9428 2271

Fax: (03) 9428 4743
Mail order, Wholesale/Retail

BEADS

Beads & Buttons Galore
28–30 Chatham St
Prahran, Vic 3181
Tel. (03) 9518 5477
Fax. (03) 9510 8477

The Bead Co.
336 Smith St
Collingwood, Vic 3166
Tel. (03) 9419 0636

Maria George
(Delica Beads)
179 Flinders Lane
Melbourne, Vic 3000
Tel. (03) 9650 1151

WOOD TURNED PRODUCTS

Susan Patten
14 Allendale Rd
Croydon, Vic 3136
Tel. (03) 9725 8476

GIMP AND RIBBON

Designer Trim
387 Bridge Rd
Richmond, Vic 3121
Tel. (03) 9428 4897
Fax. (03) 9429 2702

UK THREAD SUPPLY

Yeomans Yarns
36 Churchill Way
Fleckney
Leicestershire LE8 8UD
Tel. (0116) 240 4464
Fax. (0115) 240 2522